Ask Jackie

Pressure Canning

ISBN: 978-0-9860152-6-7

Backwoods Home Magazine

Edited by Jessie Denning, Julia Denning, Haley Kessel,
Connie Sayler, Lisa Nourse, Rhoda Denning, and Ilene Duffy
Cover art by Don Childers
Illustrations by Don Childers, Jessie Denning, and John Dean

Contents

Introduction

Pressure canning is a terrifically important homesteading skill that more and more folks are rediscovering lately. By learning how safe and easy it is to pressure can, you will open a vast array of foods to add to your pantry shelves. In any one year, I usually can ham chunks and dices, roast beef slices and dices, stewing beef, stewing venison, venison steaks and roasts, chicken breast, chicken dices, chicken chunks, three flavors of meatballs, two flavors of spaghetti sauce with meat, turkey breast slices, turkey chunks, beef broth, chicken broth, turkey broth, soups, stews, pepperoni, pizza sauce, green beans, peas, baked beans, pintos for refried beans, kidney and other dry beans, sweet corn, creamed corn, corn with peas, corn with carrots, corn with mixed vegetables, cabbage, rutabagas, potatoes, carrot slices, carrot chunks, whole carrots, squash chunks (I purée them and make pumpkin pie!), and a whole lot more. All using a pressure canner!

As pressure canning looks more involved than water bath canning, and because some folks have heard horror stories passed down through the generations about pressure canners blowing up, a lot of people are fearful to even try pressure canning. I'm here to tell you that modern pressure canners are safe and easy to use. Just follow directions and stay in the same room as your canner to monitor the pressure. No sweat. You'll be so glad you gave it a whirl!

A pressure canner is necessary for canning all low-acid foods like vegetables, meats, and combinations of the two. A boiling water bath canner never gets hot enough to kill dangerous bacteria and toxins that could possibly find their way into your low-acid foods. You must use a pressure canner and proper processing times to be safe.

Most of the information in this book pertains to pressure canning, but there could be a couple questions about water bath canning as well.

In these pages, I answer questions about such things as canning meat, dairy products, meals in a jar, vegetables, tomatoes, nuts, peppers, and a whole lot more. Have fun reading and I hope I answered a lot of your own questions along the way. — **Jackie Clay**

Dairy

Canning powdered milk

I have a question concerning canning milk. I bought milk at a good price and also powdered milk. I thought I could make up a gallon of powdered milk and combine it with a half-gallon of 2% milk and can it up in order to stretch my stores. Well, after about three months it spoiled. I used both the pressure canner and water bath. The pressure canned came out somewhat darker in color than the water bath but it all appeared okay. I put it away for a time then checked them and the milk turned almost solid in the jar, but could in some cases be jiggled back to liquid.

What did I do wrong? Was there something in the powdered milk that caused it to sour? And boy, what a smell.

Pat Fessler, Maryland

7

I honestly don't know what happened! I've never had canned milk go sour. But I've never canned any powdered milk either. (That shouldn't have had any problems.) Pressure canned milk always does get a little darker, due to the sugars in the milk getting heated to high temperatures. And it is common for it to get thicker, like condensed milk. But it shouldn't go bad!

Pressure canning milk

We will be getting a milk cow soon and are excited to use the milk for butter, cheese, etc. I would also like to can some. But I just can't find out how long to process it. Because of the acidity, I believe the only way to successfully can it would be in a pressure canner. Could you please help me?

Dianna

Milk is easy to can, but it does not come out like raw milk. It is fine to cook with, but it sort of caramelizes and gets thicker. Milk is higher in acid than one might think, containing lactic acid. So you can either pressure can it or process it in a water bath canner.

To pressure can the milk, cool your fresh, strained milk, then pour it into clean jars. Leave half an inch of room at the top of the jar. Place a hot, previously boiled lid on the jar and screw down the ring firmly tight. Process in a pressure canner for 10 minutes, at 10 pounds pressure (unless you live at an altitude requiring adjustment; see your canning manual for directions).

To water bath process your milk, simply place the jars in your hot water bath canner and process for 60 minutes, counting from the time the kettle comes to a rolling boil.

Canning milk

I have recently been trying to can milk. According to a recipe online, you can do it. This recipe has you place your milk in clean quart jars in pressure canner. Add 2-3 inches of water and get pressure to the 5 lb. mark. Then cut off heat and let steam escape. Violá, you canned milk! Well, so far, so good, until I went back to check on it a few weeks later. To my surprise, I have lots of yogurt. I kept it out of light, even storing some under the house. Temps only got from 65-80°F after cooling in house and under. My questions are these: 1)Can you successfully can milk? 2)How can you do it without getting yogurt and/or sick? I am using raw cow's milk.

Melisa Mink, Mississippi

Yes, you can home can milk. But not at 5 pounds pressure. Nor do you "cut off heat and let steam escape." Here's how I do it.

Remember that canned milk does not look or taste like fresh milk. It is a bit thicker and a little more tan in color. But it is great for cooking.

You can use the boiling water bath method by filling hot, sterilized jars with warm, strained milk. Leave ½ inch of headspace. Wipe the rim of the jar clean, place a hot, previously simmered lid on the jar, and screw the ring down firmly tight. Process quarts in a boiling water bath canner for 60 minutes.

Or you can pressure can it by filling the jars with warm, strained milk, leaving ½ inch of headspace. Wipe the rim of the jar clean, place a hot, previously simmered lid on the jar and screw the ring down firmly tight. Process quarts for 10 minutes at 10 pounds pressure in a pressure canner.

If you live at an altitude above 1,000 feet, consult your canning book for instructions on increasing your time if you water bath, or pressure if you are using a pressure canner.

Canning whole milk

I tried canning whole milk, about 10 quarts. They have all thickened up and the jars have sealed. Can I use this milk in some way? I lucked out at the time I thought, as our local grocer's ad had four gallons for $9.

Rosemary Barber, Iowa

You can use this milk in any recipes calling for milk, such as gravies, white sauces, baking, casseroles, noodle dishes, and more. I use it in place of evaporated milk, as it is thicker than regular milk.

Canning dry milk?

I just read in BHM *Issue #94 your description of how to can fresh milk. Do you know if it's possible to can reconstituted non-fat dry milk? I have **tons** of it.*

Pat Crowder, Colorado

I wouldn't bother reconstituting dry milk in order to can it. Canned milk is not really that good, except in cooking. The dry milk lasts a long time in airtight jars or even in the original boxes and doesn't take up canning jars better used for something else. Nor do they take up much room on a pantry shelf. Maybe you need to begin using the oldest milk, in order to rotate your stock. Use it in puddings, cream pies, ice milk, and custards. You can even make cheeses out of it if you want.

Powdered milk

We have a large quantity of 10-year-old powdered milk. How can we make cheese from the old powdered milk?
Carthal and Janice Hawks, South Carolina

Your milk should still be fine; dehydrated milk lasts for a long time, provided that it is kept in an airtight container. But you can make cheese from it if you'd like. In fact, you can make several types of cheese, and also yogurt, cottage cheese, and ice cream from it. Here's a basic simple cheese recipe for you.

> 4 Tbsp. plain live culture yogurt
> 1 gallon reconstituted dry milk

Mix yogurt into milk, then heat to 100°F. Wrap jar with heavy towels and leave out at room temperature until the liquid separates and a curd forms. Put into a tightly woven piece of old, clean sheet and hang so it will drip into a bowl. When it has finished dripping, turn the curd out into a bowl and add salt to taste, if desired. You can use this cheese as a spread or like

11

cream cheese. By adding chopped chives, bits of bacon, ground pineapple, etc., you can make flavored spreads that are really good. You can also let your cheese ripen by forming into a flattened round ball and laying it on a clean towel over a cake rack so the air can circulate. When it is quite firm, store in a covered container in the fridge and turn every day or two. Now you have a cheese that you can slice.

꿀 　 꿀 　 꿀 　 꿀 　 꿀 　 꿀 　 꿀

The book *Cookin' With Powdered Milk*, by Peggy Layton, has a whole lot of ideas for you on using your powdered milk.

Can I can milk bought from the store?

The reason your magazine is so appealing to us is because of the resourcefulness of your writers and subscribers.

Jim and I live in Southeast Alaska on a 1979 International school bus Jim transformed into a livable and comfortable R.V. I cook on a wood burning cook stove that also supplies our hot water and heat. We have electricity thanks to a very fuel efficient Honda gas generator. We don't own a computer and don't have a phone service and miss neither.

Is it safe to can pasteurized milk (from the store) using the water bath method?

We buy pasteurized whole milk here at our little local store for $6 a gallon. Even at that price the cost would be economical because 10 oz. cans of store brand condensed milk are $1.29 each.

Also, can I make and can a sweetened condensed milk using the store milk and the water bath method?
Do you have a recipe for this?

Jim and Shelly Isabell, Alaska

Yes, you can home can store milk. The water bath time of 60 minutes works for pints and quarts as milk is a liquid.

Yes, I have a recipe for the sweetened condensed milk, but it is in storage right now until we get our house finished, and I can't locate that box. So sorry!

Make evaporated milk from goat milk

I am a "self-taught" canner and have been putting up a variety of food for years. By the time I came along, my mother and grandmother wanted no more of canning with the exception of the occasional jams or jellies. I would like to know if there is a recipe for making evaporated milk from goat milk (naturally, using a pressure canner). We currently have three milking does, and although I make a lot of cheese, there is still a surplus. I would greatly appreciate any help you can give.

Raven Smith, Florida

You can home can milk, which turns out a lot like evaporated milk.

Simply pour your strained, warm milk into clean jars to within half an inch of the top and process in a pressure canner for 10 minutes at 10 pounds pressure or in a water bath canner for 60 minutes.

Don't forget ice cream, which makes great natural smoothies and milkshakes, cream cheese, and yogurt in all kinds of fruit flavors. Our two gallon milkers scarcely can keep up with us in the summer when so many great foods are available. I, too, make lots of different cheeses. Goats are such valuable animals on the homestead!

Canning excess goat milk

My son has been reading BHM *for about a year and the very first thing he does is read "Ask Jackie." He thinks you have all the answers to everything. So he wanted me to ask you if goat milk can be canned at home in glass jars. We are wanting to buy some dairy goats and wanted to know if we could can the excess milk to be used at a later date.*

Nancy Lynch

Boy, do I *wish* I had all the answers. But those I do manage to have, I'll happily share. You're off on a great adventure and lots of fun with your new dairy goats. They're so versatile and easy to handle and house. Yes, you can home can milk (goat or cow), and I have done it with success. But you have to know that the end result does not taste like fresh milk, rather more like condensed milk. For that reason, it is really better to have your "girls" freshen, or give birth and come into milk, at different times of the year. This ensures that you have a constant supply of fresh milk.

The process of home canning milk is simple. You can either pressure can it by simply filling the clean jars to within ½ inch of the top with freshly strained milk. Wipe the jar rims clean and dry with a clean cloth. Place hot, previously boiled lids on the jars and tighten down the ring firmly tight. Process in a pressure canner at 15 pounds for 10 minutes. Start timing only when the canner reaches 15 pounds.

Pressure canned milk will be a tannish-cream color and taste "cooked," but will be fine in all cooking or mixing with chocolate milk mix.

To water bath can your milk, fill jars in the same manner. Then place in water bath canner, on rack, and cover with hot water to an inch over the jars. Bring canner to a boil. Begin timing once canner reaches a full boil, and boil for one hour. Remove jars and place on dry folded towel to cool out of drafts for 24 hours. This milk will be a bit creamy looking and also taste "cooked," but it will be fine in all cooking or flavored drinks, such as chocolate or malted milk.

Remember that on the homestead there is no such thing as "excess" milk. Milk is only the beginning. There is ice cream, yogurts, cottage cheese, simple soft cheeses, hard cheeses, and cream cheese. Then there are the pig and calf you can raise on goat milk to butcher later for very tasty meat. And the wethers from your does that you can raise for the best chevron ever. Not to mention goat milk soap. How much fun you folks have in store for you. I'm excited, as we have a doe, due to kid in two weeks, and I can't wait to get started.

Overprocessed goat milk

We also live in northern Minnesota. We moved to the country three years ago. Best thing we could have ever done. I started canning goat milk last year and was very happy with the outcome. It is great to be able to make bread

15

in the winter with it and not have to buy. I have always had good luck canning it until today. My oldest milk was only 5 days old, but when my milk came out of the pressure canner, 3 jars were bubbling like mad and looked different (the 4 jars that looked normal were from the morning milking). As they cooled, it looked like the milk had curdled and whey was on top of the jar. Any idea what happened? I wonder if I should throw the milk to the chickens or save it and hope it will be okay.

Lori Gallagher, Minnesota

It sounds like perhaps your pressure got up a little high or you slipped and processed the milk just a little too long. When pressure canned milk does this, it often "curdles," as you described. Personally, I'd just use the milk in a casserole, providing of course that the jars are sealed and the milk smells okay when you open the jars. I don't think it's much of a problem, other than appearance.

Canning butter, cheese, and bacon

There were a few things I was wondering about. I'm sure they were covered before, but going through years of back issues, I can't find any of them. I'd like to can butter, cheese, and bacon but can't find the old articles.

Thanks a lot for all the years of good advice!

Cheryl Olson, Wisconsin

Glad to help, Cheryl. Many of us hardcore homesteaders can butter, cheese, and bacon. But just be aware that it is "experimental" canning because nobody with a degree has written anything on it. Butter is real easy to do:

I melt the butter gently in a double boiler, on my wood kitchen range so it doesn't scorch. Then I pour it into pint or half-pint hot, sterilized jars. Wide-mouth jars make it easier to get the butter out in a lump, like you'd put on a plate. But I just use what I have and put the jar on the table. So easy.

Be sure you clean the jar rims well; butter is greasy and grease can prevent jars from sealing. I process the jars for 40 minutes in a boiling water bath canner.

This butter tastes very much like fresh. I think you'll like it.

I've done cheese in both the water bath canner and pressure canner. Both turn out fine, although the pressure canned cheese is a little harder and a bit "overcooked." It tastes fine and works well for everything I've used it for. Mozzarella changes color to a cheddar yellow, although the flavor remains the same.

To prepare the cheese for canning, cut it into cubes and fill several jars which are sitting in a roasting pan full enough with water to reach the shoulders of the jars. Begin heating the pan, which starts the cheese melting. Keep packing cubes of cheese into the jars as it melts, until the melted cheese reaches ½ inch from the top of the jars.

One at a time, wipe the rim of the jars clean, then put a hot, previously simmered lid on and screw down the ring firmly tight. Place the jars into a very warm water bath canner or a warm pressure canner.

You'll water bath process the cheese for 40 minutes (pints and half-pints) or 60 minutes for quarts. If you live at an altitude above 1,000 feet, consult your canning manual for instructions for increasing your processing time to suit your altitude, if necessary.

I pressure can my cheese for 10 minutes at 10 pounds pressure (pints and half-pints). Again, if you live at an altitude above 1,000 feet, consult your canning manual for instructions on increasing your pressure to suit your altitude, if necessary.

Bacon can certainly be home canned successfully. Store bacon needs to be diced up and mixed with a recipe for successful canning, however, as it is "watery" and thinly sliced. I've bought some for 50 cents a pound! Recently, really! And I made a whole lot of baked and refried beans with the bacon, split pea soup, and mixed vegetable/bacon soup. You work with what you've got.

To just can bacon, home-smoked "real" bacon works best. I just cut chunks of a side of bacon to fit a quart jar, pack it in dry and can it up. No liquid added. You can also slice it thickly and tie it together with cotton twine so it doesn't fall apart. Then pack it dry into the jar. Bacon is processed for 90 minutes (quarts) or 75 minutes for pints. Use wide-mouth jars for ease of packing and removing the bacon from the jar when you'll be using it.

Canning butter

I have a question about canning butter. I prepare the jars as usual, melt the butter very hot, and pour the melted butter into the jars. I don't have a water bath, so I just use the pressure cooker. I bring the pressure up to 10 lbs. and then shut it off, let it cool. The jars all seal. The butter is good to use; it just tastes like melted butter. My question is, how much time is adequate to can butter to kill the bacteria for long-time storage?

Denise Grandstaff

I've never canned butter (yet), but just last fall I discovered a way to can cheese that would work just as well with butter and might result in an even better tasting end product.

I sterilize wide-mouth pint jars, then dice up cheese in roughly inch square pieces. These jars are set into a roasting pan with enough hot water in it to come nearly to the screw rim on the jars. Put the roaster on the stove, on medium heat, and add enough cheese cubes (or butter) to nearly fill the jar. As it melts, carefully add a little more at a time, until the jar is full to within half an inch of the top. All the cheese or butter is melted at this point. Then quickly wipe the jar rim clean and put hot, previously boiled lids on and screw down the ring firmly tight.

As cheese and butter are dairy products, they are acidic foods, containing lactic acid, and therefore will not support "killer bacteria" such as salmonella. So you can process the jars in a water bath canner.

I know you say you don't have a water bath canner, but I'll bet you do. Do you have any pot or kettle deep enough to fill with water an inch over your jars? A soup pot? Even a large stainless steel or aluminum mixing bowl will do. My grandmother used her copper boiler in which she used to boil water to do her laundry. You can use any such container to water bath can. The only *must*, besides water depth, is that you must keep the jars off the container's bottom to prevent the jars from breaking. Any wire rack, such as a cake cooling rack or even a folded kitchen towel, will work. It also helps if you have some sort of top for the pot; even a cookie or pizza pan will do. This gets the water boiling faster after you put your jars in.

I water bath my cheese for 40 minutes, the same as tomatoes, which are also acidic, as I have absolutely no "guide." My first batch of cheese is still sealed and tastes great when opened.

You won't die from eating "bad" cheese or butter. The worst that can happen is that it could mold (cheese) or go rancid (butter). Mine's keeping just fine, and I expect it to continue that way for a long time to come.

I don't like to experiment with canning too much. With some foods it could be dangerous. But sometimes the experts don't care much about keeping homestead produce such as cheese or butter; they're more attuned to normal canning, such as tomatoes, jam, and pickles. So we have to do the best we can, but as safely as we can.

Canned butter, bacon, and cheese shelf life

In the last two editions for Backwoods Home Magazine *I have read about how to can butter, bacon, and cheese. What is the shelf life for all?*

Lori Grieve, Iowa

As far as I know, once canned, these products remain fine for years and years. I have canned bacon, butter, and cheese and have eaten it several years later with no difference in taste or quality. Butter and cheese are still in the "experimental" canning category, but the more of us that share experiences, the better we'll be.

Canning eggs

I love to can and would like a recipe for plain canned eggs. I have your recipe for pickled eggs and they're good.
Lavada Cook, Illinois

Sorry, but there isn't a tested recipe for home canned, plain, hardboiled eggs. I wish there was!

How to can cheese

I read somewhere about you canning cheese. Now I can't find out how. Can you tell me where to look or better yet, how to do it?
Cathy Adams, Ohio

You won't find this one in a canning manual, but I experimented around and found something that works for me. One day I was canning tomatoes while whacking a chunk of cheddar cheese for "lunch." Mmm, I wondered. Tomatoes are acidic. Cheese is acidic. So I cut up cubes of cheese, sitting a wide-mouth pint jar in a pan of water, on the wood stove. Slowly cubes of cheese melted and I added more until the jar was full to within half an inch of the top. Then I put a hot, previously boiled lid on the jar, screwed down the ring firmly tight and added the cheese to a batch of jars in the boiling water bath canner to process. It sealed on removal, right along with the jars of tomatoes. Two years later, I opened it and it was great. Perhaps a little sharper than before, but *great*. So I started canning cheese of all types (but not soft cheeses) and, so far, they've all been successful. To take the cheeses out of the jar, dip the jar in a pan of boiling water for a few minutes, then take a knife and go around the jar, gently prying the cheese out. Store it in a plastic zip-lock bag.

Canning unusual items

After searching past issues, I found most of the answers to my questions on canning "unusual items." I do, however, have questions on cheese. I'm a fairly new canner and need more specific instructions.

I love this magazine and everyone's willingness to share their wealth of knowledge.

Lisa Kujawa, Indiana

I home can cheese by cutting it into one-inch cubes and placing it into wide-mouth pint jars in a roaster half filled with boiling water. As the cubes melt, I add more, stirring as needed. When the jar is filled to within ½ inch of the top, I wipe the jar rim clean and place a hot, previously simmered ring on the jar and tighten it firmly tight. The jars are then processed in a boiling water bath for 40 minutes.

To use the cheese, again heat the jar, barely melting the outside cheese, using a double boiler-type arrangement. Then, with a table knife, gently slide it around the cheese and dump it out onto a plate. It's like you'd do with Jello. Let the cheese set in a cold place to "regroup," then slice or grate and use.

I've found that the cheese may get a little stronger with long storage, but still remains good.

Using canned cheese

I read with great interest how you can cheese and how someone tried butter. My question is how do you get the cheese out of the jar? Does it stay soft, like a spread? Can you take a slice off for a sandwich? Maybe I missed something, but I can't visualize how once melted in the jar, you can get it back out, except maybe in small pieces, dug out with a knife.

Rick Murphy, Idaho

Good question, Rick. But you haven't stumped me yet. I can my cheese in wide-mouth pints and half-pints. To release the cheese, I simply heat the jar in a pan of water up to the cheese level until the outside barely melts. Sort of how you release Jell-o from a mold. Then quickly slip a thin knife in alongside the cheese to release the vacuum and dump it out on a plate. Stick it in the cold for a few minutes and you again have firm, cold cheese.

Slice or grate as you wish. I put leftovers in a plastic baggie in the fridge. This cheese isn't quite as good as fresh cheese, but it is better than store cheese, and the canned cheese is a good way to save homestead crafted cheeses over time.

Canning cheese

I did the cheese canning from your cookbook. I did mild cheddar and mozzarella. The mozzarella turned tan/ brownish and the cheddar lightened up in color. The mozzarella looks curdled. Should I not have done the mozzarella? Does the recipe only work on cheddar cheese?

Debbie Stanley, Texas

All of my cheeses have turned out very edible. The mozzarella does darken, but still works fine in recipes. Open a jar and try it. Mine tastes like pizza topping, just a little "cooked," but still yummy.

Canning cheese sauce

We are lovers of nachos of all kinds. So we buy our cheese spread in a #10 can. But sometimes it goes bad on us. Is there a way to recan the cheese spread?

Patricia Stary, California

I have recanned #10 cans of cheese spread for years successfully. But canning dairy products is still an "experimental" way of keeping them, with no official "recommended" times or methods listed. This is how I recan cheese sauce:

Gently heat a new, opened can of cheese sauce in a double boiler until simmering. Quickly ladle the hot cheese sauce out into hot, sterilized jars (I use pint and half-pint), leaving ½ inch of headspace. Carefully wipe all traces of grease off of the jar rim with a clean, hot, damp cloth. Immediately place a hot, previously simmered lid on the jar and screw the ring down firmly tight. Process in a boiling water bath for 60 minutes.

Meat

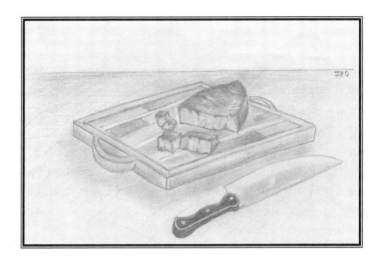

Canned meat recipes

I read with great interest your latest article on pressure canning meats.

I have pressure canned all my life, but never tried pressure canning meats because I have no recipes for using canned meat.

Can you publish some of your best recipes?

Bruce Clark, New York

You know, Bruce, I really don't use many "recipes." I'm a throw this and that together kind of person. I've cooked for so long that I've figured out how to get things to taste like I want and just do it. It drives my mother crazy. At 91, she's always used exact recipes and cringes every time I grab a handful of this or a pinch of that. Home canned meats are so easy to do and easier to use in so many ways. Basically, you use canned meat like you would any precooked meat. For instance, if you want beef stew, you just dump out a pint of canned stewing beef, a quart of tomato sauce, a pint of carrot slices, a half-pint of chopped celery, a half-pint of mushrooms, dice two large potatoes and one onion, then simmer with whatever spices you may want.

Or maybe you want barbecued beef on a bun. Take your canned stewing beef or pieces of canned beef roast and drain off the liquid into a saucepan. With a fork, shred the meat, removing any fat or gristle. (I can mine without it so it's easy to use.) Dump the meat into the saucepan with the broth and add your favorite barbecue sauce of the day to taste, then simmer for 10 minutes or longer to absorb most of the liquid; you want it thick. Pile on a bun and you've got dinner.

Chicken? Lay a bed of precooked wild rice in a baking dish. Drain a pint of canned chicken breasts onto the rice and lay the breasts neatly on it. Open a half-pint of chopped celery and sprinkle that over the chicken breasts. Add some chopped water chestnuts and grated carrot. Top with a basic poultry dressing. Cover and bake for 20 minutes.

Want a roast beef dinner? Simply open your quart of canned roast beef chunks. Arrange in a roasting pan. Add potatoes, carrots, onions, and spices. Pour the broth from the meat over the contents. Cover and roast at 350°F until the potatoes are done; add more water if necessary.

By now you get the picture. Home canned meat is so very easy to use. It makes "instant" meals that taste like you've worked for hours. That's a good thing.

Pressure canned meat

When I pressure can meat I sometimes have what I call "smoky head space" in the upper layer of double stacked pint jars. These jars are gray in the head space area. The film is on the jar and the upper layer of meat at the edges. In the past I've used it getting rid of any dark meat without ill effects. Is this wise? What causes it? Can it be prevented? If ever you do an article on meat I'd like to hear of anyone canning things such as meat loaf, etc. We love such instant meals and the tenderness of canned meat. Ham loaf has turned out well.

R. B., Ohio

I think what you are seeing is grease film, which kind of blows up along with the steam in jars of meat, leaving the meat kind of dry when out of broth or liquid in the bottom of the jar. As long as the meat was properly canned, the seals of the jars remain intact, and the meat looks and smells fine when cooked, it is safe to eat.

I just did an article on instant meals (meals in a jar) in the March/April 2008 (Issue #110). I love these canned convenience foods! We just had supper, consisting of canned meatballs, heated like meatloaf, with green peppers and tomato sauce, baked in a casserole dish. Super!

Canning meat and morels

I read your article on canning meat and was wondering about some of the things you have done. I have canned food since I was helping my mom in the early '60s. I can deer meat and beef. I have never put beef stock in jars of meat. I fill a jar with meat and place 1 bouillion cube in a pint jar and place it in canner. It always makes its own

27

juice and fat rises to top, which I remove when I open a jar. I have never browned the meat either. I have always been happy with the results. Also I have 2,000 canning jars and don't use mayo jars. I have purchased these used (for $1 a dozen) or gotten for free all of these. Most people don't want to mess with canning any more, especially city folks. It's just easier to go to McDonald's. Do you have a recipe for canning morels? I tried to freeze them once and they were not edible afterwards. If you do could you please let me know?

Rick Jahn, Indiana

Hey, if you like the results, do it that way. I did for years and years until I tried browning the meat and adding the juice. The fat rises to the top of that too, so you can remove it if you want. I find that the meat is more tender, less stringy, and more tasty. So I've pretty much switched unless I have a huge amount of meat to can. If you put your meat up raw, be sure that you preheat the meat in open jars. This is called exhausting the meat but is really warming it up before you seal the jars. Without this, you can get in trouble by not having the center of big chunks of meat hot enough during processing, which in effect cuts down the actual time your meat is processing.

Yes, morels are easy to can and taste great.

First you soak the fresh-picked mushrooms in cold, salted water to drive out any bugs. Then drain them and pat them dry with towels. Trim off any tough stems. Leave the small ones whole and slice the large ones to suit you. Simmer mushrooms in water for 5 minutes. Fill to within ½ inch of the top of the jar, using only pints and half-pints. Add salt to taste, if you wish. Fill with boiling mushroom broth to within ½ inch of the top of the jar. Process at 10 pounds pressure for 45 minutes unless you live at an altitude above 1,000 feet and must adjust your pressure to suit your altitude; check your canning manual for directions.

Canning meats

I've been cold smoking some meats before pressure canning for added flavor. I've done some with no water added and some with broth, leaving 1 inch of headspace. Is there an advantage to either method from your experiences? We're just starting to can this year. I grew up farming and banging nails, but I didn't pay attention in Mom's kitchen. She's cooking with God now, and boy do I feel dumb for not having learned about canning. I can cook, according to everyone around.

Rick Hanson, Maine

While I do can some meats, especially smoked meats, like fish, without liquid, most of my meat is canned with broth. The reason I do this is that the broth makes the texture of the meat more soft and tender, where canning dry often leaves it more stringy and "hard" textured.

Homemade mincemeat

I recently made mincemeat using a recipe from the Ball Blue Book. I followed the directions exactly but had a problem when I processed the batch.

I used a Presto 8-quart pressure canner at what I assume was 10 lbs. pressure (this model only has a weight with one setting and no gauge).

I left the proper headspace (1 inch) and processed for the time indicated. When I opened the canner, I saw that a lot of the jar contents had escaped the jar. Additionally, as the jars cooled, the contents were about half the original amount. To make matters worse, the jars did not seal and I had to freeze them.

What did I do wrong?

Max Thames, New York

Some things that can cause this to happen are: packing the food too tightly in the jars, often overfilling the jar (leaving ½ inch instead of 1 inch of headspace, for instance); varying the amount of heat under the canner; or not waiting long enough before opening the canner. With a weight control, gently bump it with a spoon. When no steam escapes, remove it and open the kettle. This loss of food from the jars often happens when someone "hurries" the cooling down period too much, sometimes by opening the petcock too soon or even by pouring cold water over the canner. This is a real *no no*. This happens, but it is not a frequent occurrence in canning, so don't let it discourage you.

Sailboat living

I moved last year onto a sailboat without refrigeration and so have learned much about canning and have successfully canned beef stew and meatballs in sauce. They were both fabulous and so welcome in chilly and damp Alaskan anchorages. I want to do so much more and hope you can advise. Four questions for you:

1) I've bought some giant jars of kalamata and marinated olives and wonder if it's safe to repackage them in half-

pint jars? Can you foresee any problems in doing this? I've heard of the FoodSaver vacuum-packer attachment specifically for mason jars and wonder if it is a necessary step. Also, could I do the same thing with the giant jars of sun-dried tomatoes packed in olive oil? I just want them accessible in smaller portions.

2) Is it possible to can sausage links? And what about Polish sausage? Or andouille? Can I just stuff them on end into pint jars, fill with liquid and pressure can? What would you advise?

3) Is there a preference safety-wise with regard to raw-packing meats or cooking them first?

4) If I wanted to prepare pints of fajita filling — steak or chicken pieces, onions, peppers, and spices, how would you recommend I proceed?

Also, I wanted to report about my visit to the Mormon cannery in Portland. The guy there was very friendly. It is available to the general public during limited hours. Groups with food to can may also use their canning facilities. Everything is in #10 cans, from freeze-dried refried beans to mashed potato pearls and dried apples (which were yummy!). They had about 20 items available. Reasonable prices. Though for my purposes, I was best off buying from the large bulk stores because I needed to re-package everything, mostly by vacuum packing. Still, I'd recommend it if storing in #10 cans suits your needs.

Thanks for all you do for us!

Susanna Sharp, Alaska

I have never canned olives, nor repackaged them; and the only reference I can find on the subject cautions strongly against it. Any readers out there with more information for

Susanna? But there is no reason that you cannot repackage your sun-dried tomatoes in oil. Simply make sure that the tomatoes are totally covered with the oil to prevent spoilage. I would pack them in sterilized jars, using sterilized lids as well, as an extra precaution. And I would use them fairly soon; they may not keep as long as canned tomatoes would. You could also consider carrying sun-dried tomatoes, alone, to add to your oil as you need them. This would require less weight and fewer jars, both a bonus on a sailboat.

Yes, you can home can sausage links and just about any other cased sausage.

Lightly brown them, then partially cook them to reduce the size. I add water to the sausage, making a flavored broth. Pack the sausage into your jars, and ladle the broth to cover up to an inch from the top of the jar. Process pints at 10 pounds pressure (unless you are canning at an elevation above 1,000 feet and must adjust your pressure to match your elevation; consult your canning manual for instructions) for 75 minutes and quarts for 90 minutes.

The only problem I've encountered in canning cased sausage is that sometimes they tend to swell under pressure. This does not affect the taste, only the appearance. When you open a jar and cook up the sausage, this swelling is not so apparent.

As to the safety of raw packed meat, as long as you cut your chunks of meat into one inch slices and use hot broth ladled over it, raw meat will can up just as safe as precooked meat. In older canning manuals, and as I've done myself, meat was just cut into convenient chunks and packed into jars without the hot broth. But, this meat was preheated by placing the open jars in a roasting pan with enough water in it to come up to the neck of the jar, but not boil into the jar. The roaster was put into the oven at a low temperature. A meat thermometer was periodically inserted into the center of one of the middle jars. Before the jars were removed and a hot, previously simmered lid put on, the temperature of the meat had to reach at least 170°F. Unfortunately, many people shortcutted this process and the meat did not reach a high enough temperature for long enough (in the canner) to provide safety against harmful bacteria.

So this process has largely fallen by the wayside in favor of precooking the meat. The reason I, personally, precook the meat is that more meat fits in a jar and that meat has a more tender texture on using it later. It also has a prettier appearance in the jar.

If I were making fajita filling to can, I'd precook the steak or chicken pieces, making a good batch of broth with it, including the spices you prefer. Then I would add the chopped vegetables and stir the batch well and immediately add the hot mixture to your hot pint jars and cap. As meat is an ingredient in fajita mix, you would process the pints at 10 pounds pressure (see altitude adjustment directions above) for 75 minutes.

Canning ham

I know you have talked about canning store-bought ham in the past, but I can't find any instructions from you

*about how to do it. With the holidays upon us, hams are
relatively inexpensive, and I'd like to try to can some ham.*

Dallen Timothy, Arizona

The way I do ham is to heat the ham in a roasting
pan until warm throughout. Then I cut the ham into
one-inch slices, chunks, or dices and pack hot into
hot jars, leaving 1 inch of headspace. I make a ham
broth or just pour boiling water over the ham, leaving
1 inch of headspace. Wipe the rim of the jar clean,
place a hot, previously simmered lid on the jar, and
screw down the ring firmly tight. Process half-pints
and pints for 75 minutes and quarts for 90 minutes
at 10 pounds pressure in a pressure canner. (Altitude
adjustments possible over 1,000 feet; consult your canning manual.)

This ham is great and I use it every week. I'm buying it
on sale right now, too.

Preserving bacon and canning ham

*How do you preserve bacon? Is there a way to can or dry
it? I would like to buy a fresh pig and it would be cut up.
I planned on canning most of it. But what about ham or
bacon?*

Kathy Lupole, New York

While I have canned bacon, we usually just have our hogs
butchered and hung up during quite cold fall weather. When
the hams and bacon are finished smoking I hang the bacon,
covered with cheesecloth, from wires in an unheated attic.
Perhaps one ham is hung with it, while the rest is cut up and

canned. The unheated attic was usually about 35°F on average and the ham and bacon kept just fine until we ate it up.

The ham, I slice, debone, and slightly pan fry, then add enough water to make a broth to cover the slices in wide-mouth canning jars. Some of the ham I dice into one-inch cubes to use in mixed dishes such as scalloped potatoes and ham or ham and beans.

I place the slices or cubes of ham in the canning jars to within an inch of the top, then pour on the hot broth, covering the meat to within an inch of the top. The jars are processed for 90 minutes at 10 pounds pressure unless you live at an altitude requiring adjustment of the pressure. Read your canning manual for instructions.

Canning bacon

I am wanting to can some bacon and homemade butter. I read your column on canning meats and bacon wasn't mentioned. I would really appreciate knowing how to do this as soon as possible.

Another question I have is concerning our turkey that we canned in a pressure cooker. I know in a water bath that you only screw on the lid till it meets first resistance, or so I have been told. But what about in a pressure cooker? When we pressured the turkey, a lot of the broth oozed out of the jars. Did I not get the lids tight enough? And also, I was canning at 12 lbs. pressure because we live at 2,000 feet, and sometimes it went up to 13. What happens if we can a little higher pressure, does it hurt the food and can we have too much pressure?

Thank you so much for answering my questions. I haven't pressured food for 20 years and have forgotten a lot of it, even though we had the gauge checked at the extension office.

Linda Monfort, Washington

I recently talked about canning bacon on my blog, but here's the basics, in case you missed it. I can mostly home-smoked sides of bacon; they're firmer and not as fatty. You can also can "store" bacon, but the pieces that are not sliced can up much nicer than regular sliced bacon. At any rate, try to get bacon that is as lean as possible.

I put my bacon in a roasting pan, in the oven, and roast at 250°F until it shrinks some, heating through-out. Then I cut it into jar-sized pieces and pack hot into hot wide-mouth jars. I add no liquid. Bacon is processed for 75 minutes for pints and 90 minutes for quarts, at 10 pounds pressure. (Adjust for altitudes above 1,000 feet above sea level.)

Another way I can bacon is to use it in other recipes that I can. For instance, I can baked beans, split pea soup, and vegetable mixes that include precooked bacon pieces. This works very well for less than ideal store bacon. I recently got 20 pounds of bacon at the store for 50 cents a pound (nearly outdated). I canned a lot of that up in baked beans, split pea soup, and pintos. It worked great and tastes ter-rific.

You got your jar lids on tight enough. Liquid blowing out of the jar happens during canning. It does not affect the quality of the food. It can happen from filling the jar too full, opening the canner before the pressure is totally down to zero, or having the pressure fluctuating suddenly. I don't think going up to 13 pounds had anything to do with it. But in any case, don't worry, as long as the jars sealed. No, it doesn't hurt to have the pressure a little higher, but just right is best as the food doesn't overcook.

Canned bacon

I have a question about canned bacon. I love to can, even though I have little time. But when I saw the instructions for canning bacon, it made me want to try it! I am wondering, do you add water to the jar after you put the rolled up bacon in? I didn't see that in the instructions, but then I'm wondering what keeps the jars from breaking when they are under pressure?

Mary Ann Winders, Kentucky

No, you don't add water to the bacon. Quite a few smoked foods are canned with no water added. The jars will not break under pressure. The liquid is to keep the food moist and help the heat penetrate into the center of the canned food. But bacon isn't that dense a product.

"Bolos" Texas beef jerky

I'm looking for a recipe called "Bolos" Texas Beef Jerky. It is tube bologna that is pickled with onions, carrots and peppers. You can get it hot or mild.

I have found some recipes for pickling bologna, but I'm concerned because it says boil your first five ingredients then pour over your bologna and onions in a jar and then place in refrigerator.

I want something that can be canned indefinitely and stored in the cabinet. If you could help with this, it would be greatly appreciated.

Cecilia Rowe

If you are satisfied with the recipe you found, simply use that recipe and then can your bologna in wide-mouth pint jars, taking care to heat the packed open jars in a roaster pan full of water. The water should be to within an inch of the top of the jar. This is called "exhausting," but is really preheating before you cap the jars and place them in a pressure canner. It is meant to bring the internal temperature of the meat up to 190°F before it goes in to begin processing. You can heat this roaster full of open jars on your stove top or in the oven and test the internal temperature of your meat with a kitchen thermometer.

When the meat is evenly heated, seal the jars and process in a pressure canner for 90 minutes. The USDA now recommends that high density foods, such as bologna, not be home canned. I can only say I've done it for years and am still living. I do exhaust my jars of dense meat.

Canned meatball recipe

Will you please share the recipes for your meatballs and the different sauces you have canned them in? I have been canning everything I can get my hands on, since buying my first pressure canner this spring, and have enjoyed every minute. If it can't get away from me, I put it in a jar. I love hearing those lids ping and pop! Since I'm starting out new, I've had to purchase jars, but our local Ace Hardware is selling them for $7.00 a dozen until the end of August, so each payday I buy a few more. Everyone else is selling

*them for $12, so I'm getting as many as possible from Ace.
I just wanted to say thank you for encouraging people to
try new things. I'm having such a wonderful time.*

Rosemarie Wesolek, Pennsylvania

I'm having fun canning right now. I first made meatballs,
using institutional sized cream of mushroom soup, diluted
with water mixed with the drippings from the pan I cooked
the meatballs in. I was frying my meatballs in two frying
pans, but a friend told me she put hers into a roasting pan
and baked them. They brown on all sides with no fussing
around or turning them over all the time. I did that today
and it worked great! My meatballs in mushroom sauce goes
like this:

I used 10 pounds of hamburger (on sale, of course!).
To that, I mixed 1 cup chopped onions, 1 Tbsp. black
pepper, and 4 Tbsp. seasoning salt. I smushed that in
well with my hands and formed up the meatballs. You
can also mix in cracker crumbs or oatmeal and eggs,
like you do meatloaf, if you wish. Bake the meatballs
in roasting pans at 350°F, until just done; they shrink
down. Pour off most of the grease. Dip the meatballs
out with a wooden spoon and gently slip into wide-
mouth canning jars. While the meatballs are baking,
heat 2 family sized or 1 institutional sized can of cream
of mushroom soup and half a can of water in a large
saucepan to nearly boiling. Add your pan drippings,
diluted with another half can of water. Pour this into
your mushroom soup and mix well. Ladle this over
your meatballs, to within 1 inch of the top. Process
at 10 pounds pressure for 90 minutes for quarts or 75

minutes for pints. If you live at an altitude over 1,000 feet, consult your canning manual for instructions on adjusting your pressure to suit your altitude.

Today I made meatballs with green peppers and onions with tomato sauce. I simply added chopped green peppers to the other recipe and mixed in well, topping the full jars with home canned tomato sauce from last season.

Tomorrow, I'm making Italian meatballs, using garlic, onion, basil, and oregano and using the tomato sauce. Instant spaghetti meatballs! It's so fun!

Remember, all meat products are processed for the same time, so you can use any recipe you like.

Oops — waterless canning

Read your stuff all the time. I just did a really stupid thing and need your advice.

I am pressure canning some beef, and it's far from my first time. It was while I was unloading the first 14 pints that I realized that I never put water in the canner. The jars have all sealed, the canner stayed in one piece, but I'm wondering if the meat will be okay. What do you think?

Mary Wolfe, Pennsylvania

Wow! That's a new one on me! Here's my guess: probably, your meat is okay, as the jars have all sealed and there probably was some steam generated by moisture in the jars during processing. But I'd mark the jars and be awful sure I checked each one carefully upon use. Look at the meat, open a jar, making sure it is still sealed well, then smell the meat. If all is okay, be sure to bring the meat to boiling temperature for 15 minutes before eating.

I'll bet you never do that again. How scary! I have visions of a warped canner and blowing up jars!

Canning sausage, wieners, and bacon

Would you be so kind as to ask Jackie Clay how to can wieners and link sausage you buy from the store? I'd like to give it a try.

Elaine Hales, Texas

Do you can sausage and bacon?

Nancy Green

Yes, you can home can link sausage and wieners, as well as bacon. I often do it when we butcher or get wieners on sale. You can also can any other store-bought or home-made sausage, such as salami, pepperoni, bologna, etc.

The only problem with canning sausage or wieners in a casing is that often the meat will swell, splitting the casing, which does nothing to hurt the taste or edibility of the product but it will result in a visually less appealing product.

When canning any sausage in a casing, pack them cold in a clean pint jar, upright, and as snug as you can get them without force. Use no liquid. If you use liquid, they will swell much worse, and some of the liquid will boil out during the processing, possibly resulting in an incomplete seal.

Wipe the jar rim with a clean cloth, put on lids which have been boiled in water and are still warm, then tighten rings down firmly. Process in pressure canner only for 75 minutes. If you use quarts, process for 90 minutes at 10 pounds of pressure. (If you're more than

41

1,000 feet above sea level, see your canning book for altitude adjustments.)

When canning bacon, it's best to use only lean bacon, either unsliced or sliced but kept in one chunk, and trimmed to fit into the jar you will be using, either pint or quart.

You'll find that wide-mouth jars work best. Be sure to leave an inch of headroom above the bacon. Pack the uncooked bacon in the jar snugly, then seal and process as above.

I've found it better to can sausage patties, rather than link sausage, just for visual effect. Besides, you don't have to use casing if you are making your own from home grown pork or venison.

Simply fry the patties lightly, browning them a bit. Add a small amount of water to the sausage fat. Lift sausage patties and stack to within an inch of the top of the jar. Then add about 4 tablespoons of the juice to each jar. Wipe rims, put on lids, and screw bands down firmly. Process pints for 75 minutes and quarts for 90 minutes. The basic pressure for all meat is 10 pounds, but adjust the pressure upward for elevations over 1,000 feet.

Home canning sausage

I would like to know if I can home can frozen sausage patties bought from the store. If so, how do we do this? I have read that sage may make the homemade sausage patties bitter. The frozen patties I am asking about do have some sage in them. I would like to can them though because of freezer space. I can get a couple hundred frozen uncooked sausage patties really reasonable.

Wanda, Ohio

I doubt that the small amount of sage in frozen sausage patties will make them bitter. I always go light on the seasonings when canning seasoned sauces and meats, as the canning and storage does intensify the spices. Your best bet is to can a pint or two of the brand of sausage patties you like and open them a while later and see how they turned out. When I can my sausage patties, I lightly fry them up. This shrinks them in size and also makes them taste better on opening the jar.

Canning sausage

I just placed my order for fresh sausage from a local meat processor. I love canned sausage and have done it in the past by raw packing. I was reading over the instructions in your canning book and was wondering if there is a particular reason you prefer browning your sausage first. My first thought was that raw pack might not be considered safe canning practice any more, but I thought I'd ask.

Marlana Ward, Tennessee

I used to raw pack my sausage and meat, then I found that when I lightly browned it and then added water to the pan drippings to make a broth, the resulting meats were more tender and flavorful. With ground meats, packing raw meat into a jar and then processing it could result in a too-dense product where the heat needed for safe processing might not reach the center of the jar for a long enough

43

time. So if you make patties from your sausage, lightly brown them, then stack them in a jar with a little broth; there is room for the steam to heat between the patties as well as over and around the outside of the jar.

Canning "pizza" sausage

I just recently bought a very large bag of pizza sausage (the little sausage balls found on pizzas). Can they be canned into smaller amounts? Like pints or half-pints? I think they may get freezer burned before I use them all. If so, how would I go about doing that?

Joni Warren, Oregon

Yes, you can! What I would do is to thaw the sausage, then warm it in the oven, on a cookie sheet. Don't "cook" it, just heat it well. Gently pack into half-pint or pint jars, then cover with boiling water, leaving 1 inch of headspace. Process pint and half-pint jars for 75 minutes at 10 pounds in a pressure canner. If you live at an altitude above 1,000 feet, consult your canning book for directions on increasing your pressure to suit your altitude.

Bologna and corned beef recipes

Thank you for answering my questions on smoked fish and baked beans canning. You mentioned you can bologna and corned beef. Would you please share the recipe?

James R. Coffey, Maryland

Glad I was of help. That's what I'm here for, after all. And the more people I can help out, the better, as far as I'm concerned. As for the recipes, here are two that work for us:

Home canned bologna:

> 25 lbs. fresh ground meat
> 1 lb. Morton Tender Quick
> 1 tsp. garlic powder
> 4 tsp. liquid smoke
> ½ tsp. saltpeter
> ¾ cup brown sugar
> 1 oz. coarse ground black pepper

Grind the meat twice, adding spices etc., as you grind, and mix well. Put in an enameled turkey roaster, covered, and let set in a cool place for three days. A refrigerator works fine. Grind again and pack into wide-mouth pint jars to within an inch of the top. Wipe the rims clean and place a previously boiled, warm lid on the jar and screw down the ring firmly tight. Place in a pressure canner and process for 90 minutes at 10 pounds, adjusting the pressure as needed to allow for altitude. (Check your canning book for these adjustments.)

This bologna is very good and doesn't taste like "store" bologna (which we hate). It kind of tastes like a cross between good liver sausage and corned beef. We like it sliced from the jar and fried. I hope you'll like it, too.

Home canned corned beef:

To corn the beef, choose well-chilled beef and remove all the bones. You may use the brisket, rump, or chuck roasts. Cut the meat into uniform pieces and weigh the

45

entire pile. Allow 2 to 2½ pounds of salt for every 25 pounds of beef. Sprinkle a layer of salt on the bottom of a crock. Place a layer of meat in the crock and add more salt. Continue packing in this manner until all the meat has been packed. Cover the top layer with a good layer of salt.

Allow the packed meat to remain in the salt for 24 hours, in a cool place, covered to prevent debris and insects from falling into the crock. Then cover the salted meat with this solution:

> 2 lbs. sugar
> 2 oz. saltpeter
> 1 oz. baking soda
> 2 gallons of water

Make a spice bag containing 1 ounce pickling spices and two or more (to taste) crushed cloves of garlic. Place the bag in the brine with the meat. Be certain that all the meat is completely covered with brine. Place a china plate on top and weigh it down to keep the meat submerged.

The meat is cured for 30 days at 38° to 40°F. If the temperature gets warmer, the brine will get ropy, which means that it feels snotty and stringy when you dip your finger into the brine. If this should happen, immediately drain all the brine and rinse the meat well. Throw away the old brine and make new brine and cover. Be sure to check your pickling meat often, especially if the temperature fluctuates and could go above 40°.

At the end of the brining period, remove the meat from the brine, rinse well, and drain. Pat it dry with a clean towel.

To can the corned beef, soak the meat for two hours in clean water, then boil it slowly in clean water for 30 minutes. Remove the meat from the boiling water and cut it into pieces that will pack into wide-mouth pint or quart jars. Pack the jars to within an inch of the top of the jar. Add liquid, in which the meat was boiled, to within an inch of the top. Wipe the rim of the jar clean. Place previously boiled jar lids in place and screw down ring firmly tight. Process in your pressure canner for 90 minutes at 10 pounds pressure, adjusting pressure if necessary to make allowances for altitude. (See your canning book for instructions.)

This corned beef is very good and tender. I hope you will like it.

Canning meat

I have written to you before and found your advice to be invaluable. I have a canning question. My hubby and I raise both ducks and chickens. What is the best way to can meat? We tried one way and found that mold grew inside the jars. We think it happened because of the amount of fat that wound up in the jar. Do you have any advice regarding this? We have limited freezer space and we're told canning the meat keeps it tender.

Jaime Hogsett, Wisconsin

Yes, canning meat does make it tender … and convenient, too. If mold grew inside of the jars, either the meat was canned in a water bath canner or was not properly pressure canned.

I can all my meat by first cooking it (with chickens or duck, usually boiling it till tender), then skimming the fat off. I pack the hot meat into the hot jars, then pour broth over it to within an inch of the top of the jars. Hot, previously simmered lids are put on the jar rims, which have been wiped clean of broth and grease, and the rings screwed down firmly tight. Process meat for 90 minutes (quarts) or 75 minutes (pints) and poultry for 75 minutes (quarts) or 65 minutes (pints), at 10 pounds pressure. If you live at an altitude above 1,000 feet, consult your canning manual for directions on increasing your pressure to suit your altitude.

Are you sure there was mold on your meat, in the jars? Solid fat is white and can look a lot like mold in jars unless you are used to canning. Were the jars still sealed? Did the meat smell okay? When meat goes bad, where there is mold, it usually stinks like crazy. If you canned it properly and the seals were still good, I'd suspect your mold was, in fact, just solidified grease.

Butchering old hens

I am getting ready to butcher old hens. I have some that are more than 3 years old. Will they tenderize as I pressure can them or am I wasting my time? Do you precook them?

Cindy Hills, Wisconsin

Your hens will give you great meat. Yes, it will become tender during pressure canning. Even old roosters make great, flavorful meat. I do precook my chickens, regardless of age, for ease of packing the jars and a more appetizing end product.

Canning chicken

I would like to know if I could can chicken with bones (like drumsticks, thighs, etc.). I usually freeze it, but recently we suffered a power outage and I had to throw out a lot of food from my freezer. P.S. I am writing by candlelight. Our power is still off! This makes day #4.

Sarah Funk, West Virginia

You are experiencing one of the "emergencies" that most of us, sooner or later, experience. Maybe it's not as dramatic as terrorists and smallpox, but to you, when it's happening, it's pretty much an emergency. Which is just why I've preached preparedness for a long, long time.

I too, lost a good part of my huge freezerful due to a lengthy power outage, which is why I don't have one now. I dry or can most everything including chicken and other poultry, complete with the bones. This is really a time saver when we are butchering chickens, as it allows me to can many more birds in a day than I could possibly do if I deboned them all. And, as a bonus, you can debone the canned chicken at a later date, saving the bones to boil up with some of the lesser parts, such as the backs, wings, and skin, to make a dynamite soup stock with the same jars of chicken that your stir fried dish or barbecued chicken came from.

Canning chicken and pheasants

*I'm new to canning and am looking to can chicken &
pheasants in pints and quart jars. Could you help with
pressure and time for this?*

Scott Pharo, Wisconsin

Raw packed (bone in or not) chicken and pheasant, with
hot broth or boiling water poured to within 1 inch of the
top of the jar, should be processed at 10 pounds pressure
(unless you live at an altitude above 1,000 feet and must
consult a canning manual for directions in raising your
pressure if necessary), boned pints for 75 minutes, or 90
for quarts; bone-in pints for 65 minutes, or 75 for quarts.

For hot pack, where you can partially cooked chicken or
pheasant, use the same times as above, with hot broth or
boiling water (doesn't taste as good) to 1 inch of the top of
the jar, as well. The pressure is the same.

Canning turkey a la king

*I am new to canning. I would like to can some turkey a la
king made with cream of mushroom soup and veggies. If I
put milk in it, is it safe to eat? I am using a pressure canner. I thought it might go bad with milk in it.*

Dave Roberts

No, putting milk in your turkey a la king won't make it go
bad. But the end result of any milk gravy type foods is that
the milk appears curdled in the finished product. It tastes
okay, but looks yucky. Because of this, I omit the milk, using a broth/flour gravy, then add milk when I heat up the
jar of food. Here is one recipe that works well for me.

Turkey à la king:

> 5 lbs. bone-in turkey
> 3 quarts water
> 4 Tbsp. flour
> 1 Tbsp. salt
> 1 quart turkey broth or chicken soup base
>   equivalent
> 1 cup mushrooms, chopped
> 2 chopped red bell peppers
> 1 chopped green pepper
> 2 tsp. black pepper

Cut the turkey into pieces. Place in large pot with 3 quarts water and cook until tender. Cool, then remove meat from bones and cut into small pieces. Dissolve flour and salt in a little of the cold broth to make a paste and add to the remainder of the quart of broth which has been heated. Cook until slightly thickened, stirring to keep free of lumps. Add mushrooms, peppers, and black pepper. Heat to boiling and fill clean canning jars to within one inch of the top of the jar. Wipe jar rim clean with damp cloth. Place hot, previously boiled lid on and screw down ring firmly tight. Process in pressure canner for 90 minutes at 10 pounds unless your altitude requires more pressure. (See your canning manual for directions.)

When you heat this up, it will be thick, and you may now add milk to your taste. Good eating. This is one of my favorite ways to get rid of excess holiday turkey.

Canning salmon

How do you can smoked salmon?

James Coffey, Maryland

Smoked salmon is easy to can. We also smoke and can a number of other fish which also taste great, including trout, whitefish, panfish, and even the lowly sucker which is really good smoked.

Smoke the fish, using your favorite recipe, then cut into jar-sized pieces. Place dry into pint jars; we use wide-mouth jars for ease of packing and getting the delicate smoked fish out of the jars. If the fish seems a bit bland, I sometimes sprinkle a bit of brown sugar or salt on it, but this is seldom necessary if your smoking was done correctly. Leave 1 inch of headroom.

Wipe the jar rims. Place a boiled lid on and tighten the ring firmly. Process in a pressure canner for 1 hour and 40 minutes at 10 pounds pressure (adjust for higher altitudes, if necessary).

To be absolutely safe, heat in oven at 250°F for half an hour in a covered casserole dish, then cool before eating; we just give it the sniff & appearance test, never having had bad results.

Canning raw salmon

I live in S. Central Alaska, where we eat a lot of salmon. I can raw salmon by exhausting jars in boiling water for 10 minutes before placing on lids and pressure canning. My husband says this step is unnecessary, disregarding what all my canning books say. His grandma, a wonderful woman who has been canning for 60 years, does not take

*this extra step. She also reuses lids ... something I refuse to
do. Please help settle this disagreement. "Grandma never
had any problems," my husband says. I say Grandma was
damn lucky!*

Kate McLaughlin, Alaska

This is a case where you both are right. Really. While
you can safely can salmon without exhausting (heating the
meat) before canning it, you must make sure you thoroughly exhaust steam from your canner, meaning that the canner full of cold meat has had enough time to heat, through
and through. This is especially important when you are
canning thick salmon steaks in quart jars. The contents of
pint jars take much less time to heat, through and through,
than do quart jars. If the petcocks or vent is closed too soon
(before forceful streams of steam exit them for 10 minutes),
the processing time will be inadequate. Thus your salmon
could be in danger of spoiling.

I can salmon without liquid, just the brine-rinsed steaks,
packed into hot jars, with a teaspoon of salt.

When canning salmon, it is safest to use pint jars, but I've
used quarts for years, just being sure that my canner took
enough time to thoroughly heat its contents before I began
processing. I usually add just a little extra water to the canner to allow for this extra heating up time; you don't want
your canner to steam dry.

As for reusing lids ... hmm ... well, in an emergency, it
can be done — kind of. By gently pulling the lids off some
jars, with the fingers, instead of a can opener, you can usually re-use them for jams, jellies or pickles; high-acid foods
only. I sure wouldn't reuse them for vegetables, meat, or
fish. That's a wee bit terrifying.

Pressure canning salmon

I have hot water bath canned tomatoes and jams, froze veggies and meats for years. Due to old stories, though, I have been afraid to try my hand with a pressure canner. I have finally caved in and bought a 20-quart pressure canner and would like to know about canning salmon. We catch quite a bit of this fish and halibut, as well, living here in Alaska. I would like to preserve it in jars.

Lissa Ryan, Alaska

Congratulations. I'm so glad you gave in and are willing to conquer your fears of pressure canning. There's really nothing to it if you simply get a good canning manual and follow the directions, step by step. I can most of my fish "plain" and do the recipe thing after storage.

Salmon and other fish are easy to put up. And once you try it, I'm sure you'll go on to can meat and poultry, too. Living in Alaska, you need to try canning moose. It's our favorite meat.

Can only fish that is very fresh and has been promptly cleaned and held on ice until processing, as fish is one of the foods that can be dangerous to improperly can, due to the risk of botulism. Only can fish in pint or smaller jars to ensure that the entire contents of the jar are heated thoroughly and sufficiently.

The basic process is simple. Clean and draw the fish thoroughly. Make a brine of one cup salt to one gallon of fresh, cold water. Cut the fish into jar-length pieces (remembering that you must leave one inch of headroom, that is, air space at the top of the jar). Let stand in the brine for one hour. Drain well. Pack fish into hot jars, skin side next to the glass. Wipe the jar rim well. Place hot, previously boiled lid on jar and screw down ring firmly tight. Process pints for 100 minutes at 10 pounds pressure, adjusting the pounds of pressure needed if your altitude is greater than 1,000 feet. See your canning manual for altitude adjustments.

The Division of Fishery Industries, United States Department of Interior, Washington, D.C. can provide you with many seafood canning recipes. Good canning and write if you have any questions as you go along.

Canning smoked salmon

I don't have a smoker to smoke my salmon, however, I want the smoked flavor and was wondering if I could just add liquid smoke to my fresh salmon that I want to can? If I can do this how much would I add to a pint jar?

Any information on how to can salmon would be very helpful to me.

Beulah Fern, Oregon

No, this will not give you the results you want. The liquid smoke might (or might not!) give you the flavor you want, but it won't give you the dry texture you will crave in your faux smoked salmon. If you can't afford a smoker (and they are getting cheaper and cheaper), you can simply build your own out of any container that will hold smoke. I built mine out of an old clothes dryer cabinet.

A simple rack can be fashioned out of wires strung across the inside top of the metal cabinet, barrel, or whatever your "smoker cabinet" consists of. You can hang pieces of fish on heavy wire hooks or lay them across the wires to smoke.

My smoking unit consisted of an old hot plate with an old cast iron frying pan on top of it. I set it on low and tossed a couple handfuls of hardwood chips in the frying pan and shut the door. You can use fruit wood, such as apple, cherry, or pear, if you have it, or whatever local wood is available from mesquite to birch or alder.

You will have to keep adding the wood chips as they char away. You don't want a hot smoke, only a smoky smoke.

Canning tuna

Hi Jackie, I really enjoy your column, especially the canning info. I was wondering if you could tell me the best way to can tuna. There are two methods people seem to use around here. One involves baking the tuna first before processing in a pressure canner. The other, the tuna is packed raw into jars with a pinch of salt and then processed.

Mary Griswold

You can use either method to can tuna. Let me throw in a caution here about canning any fish or shellfish. Folks, including me, have been canning fish for a long time and we've enjoyed a huge success. But, because of its nature and tendency to spoil easily, it is not recommended by experts to home can fish. That said, I personally can my fish raw, with only a little salt. It's safest to use only half-pint and pint jars, to ensure that the center of this dense meat gets hot enough during the processing. In the same vein, it's best to exhaust the open jars of fish before sealing them. This means to fill a turkey roaster or some other large pan with boiling water to such a level that when you place your filled, but not capped, jars of fish in it the water level comes halfway up the jars. Then boil this on the stove until a meat thermometer placed in the center of a center jar reads 170°F. Then quickly wipe the jar lids and place on each jar a hot, previously boiled new lid and screw down the ring firmly tight. Process pints for 90 minutes at 10 pounds pressure (unless you live at an altitude above 1,000 feet — then read your canning manual for instructions).

Canning lobster

I am an avid fisherman and have been canning tuna for many years. I have just started a lobster business and have many lobster that are not selling. So what I was looking to do is can the meat for lobster salad during the long cold winter months. Can you tell me the best way to do this?

Capt. Charlie Biddle, New York

Sure, Captain. To can lobster:

Cook and remove the meat. Pack into hot half-pint jars while meat is still quite hot. Cover with a boiling brine made up of 1 quart water and 1 tsp. pickling salt. Leave ½ inch of headspace. Place hot jars in a roasting pan with enough boiling water in it to come up to the halfway mark on the jars and boil the pan for 10 minutes. Put a cooking thermometer into the center of one of the middle jars and see if it reads 170°F. If not, continue boiling until it does. This ensures that the meat is hot, through and through, when put into the pressure canner.

Put hot, previously simmered lids on jars and screw down rings firmly snug. Process at 10 pounds pressure for 70 minutes.

Now you have lobster for your enjoyment all winter. Remember, though, when you go to use it, check each jar, then bring the contents to boiling and boil for 15 minutes for safety's sake. Then you can cool, refrigerate, and use cold.

Canning clam chowder

Is it possible to pressure can clam chowder?
Mari Ashworth, Washington

You can home can the clams in a salted, seasoned brine, but because clam chowder has milk in it, I just don't like the way it cans up. I prefer to just can the clams (if you're lucky enough to live where you can get them) alone, then just put the chowder together as you want to fix it. It only takes a few minutes with the canned clams.

Canning liver

I was wondering how you can liver. I have a lot of frozen beef and pork liver that my family isn't about to eat. I want to can it up to use for the animals, if need be, and wondered if I should cut it up small first, or leave in larger pieces. I have a lot of experience canning, and have all the equipment. I have canned meat before, but never liver. Just wondering how you would do it.

Jenny

I would slice the raw, thawed liver into one inch pieces and pack into jars, to within one inch of the top. Add no salt or liquid. Wipe the top of the jar clean and place a hot, previously boiled lid on jar and screw down ring firmly tight. Process pints for 1 hour and

15 minutes, quarts for 1 hour and 30 minutes, at 10 pounds pressure. Adjust pressure, if necessary, according to altitude; check your canning manual. You must use a pressure canner.

You could, if you wish, dice the liver instead of slicing it. Cats or small dogs would be able to eat it easier. But bigger dogs will just wolf down such a delectable treat!

Be sure you allow your canner to exhaust adequately, giving the meat time to warm up, before you close off your petcocks or steam vents. Otherwise it will not process long enough to kill harmful bacteria. Ten minutes of exhausting forceful steam is generally adequate.

Half-gallon jars and liver recipes

I have several half-gallon jars I would like to use for meal-in-a-jar (veggie beef soup, beef stew, chili, etc). Everything would be cooked, just "left-over." How do you process your jars after you fill them with soups or stews?

Also, do you have any recipes for liver (canning and eating)? All I know is liver and onions.

Bonnie Atkinson, West Virginia

It is now recommended that we do not can meats in half-gallon jars. I, along with thousands of other home canners, used to do just that with no ill effects, but there is a chance that the center of a jar of rather thick stew, chili, or whatever may not get hot enough for safe processing. So use your half-gallon jars for fruit juices, pickles, or food storage.

As for the liver and onions, sorry, but that's my only recipe; I'm not a huge liver fan, so I haven't taken it farther than that. To can it, simply slice your liver, sauté it with onions, then pack hot into hot jars, making a broth with the onions and pan drippings.

Pressure canning rabbit paté

I'm going to be butchering a multitude of rabbits soon. I haven't been using the liver when I've butchered one or two rabbits. But this time I've got a population explosion to deal with and it seems like a waste to feed that much liver to the cats. I'd like to make a liver paté, similar to chicken liver paté. My question is: can this be pressure canned? Salmon sized jars would be the ideal size. Have you done anything similar?

Karen Farmer, British Columbia

I haven't done rabbit paté, but I've made homemade bologna and corned beef, etc., and paté will can up just as nicely. I'd suggest using half-pint or smaller jars, making a "one sitting" use out of a jar. You won't be using a quart at a time, and you don't want to ruin it by leaving it too long in the fridge.

Simmer the livers in just enough water to cook them without scorching. Add salt and any other spices to taste. After they're done, put them through a food grinder or food processor at a fine grind. Then regrind the meat. If the texture pleases you, go ahead with the processing. If it seems too dry, add a bit of the broth from boiling, mixing well until the desired consistency is reached. Pack fairly tightly into small canning jars and add just enough broth that they were simmered in to barely cover the meat. Your jars should be filled up to within ½ inch of the top. Wipe the top and place warm, previously boiled lid in place. Then screw the ring down firmly tight. Process 75 minutes at 10 pounds of pressure (adjust pounds of pressure, if necessary, for all altitudes over 1,000 feet above sea level).

Check a canning book for further details of the canning process.

Canning game and domestic meat

What about canning meat? This would be game as well as domestic meat. What's a good book on canning?

John Smith

Sure, John, you can home can meat. I can all types of wild game, from elk to trout, as well as beef, poultry, etc. You can check out my article, *Canning 101*, in back issues of *BHM*. It covers meat as well as most everything one would can. A good, cheap book on canning is the *Ball Blue Book*, available wherever canning supplies are sold, even Wal-Mart. For a more extensive book (get a fairly recent one), check out your library, including the interlibrary loan. Look through a couple, and then order one that appeals to you from a nearby bookstore.

Canning meat in half-pints

In Issue #93 you talk about canning meat (deer) in half-pints or smaller. I had contacted the extension office about doing just that and they told me not to can that way. I live alone and can't use a pint of meat at one time. If you would tell me how to convert meat canning to half-pints or smaller I would be eternally grateful.

Chalice Call, Idaho

You've *got* to be kidding! Since when is canning in smaller jars *more* dangerous than in pints? Smaller jars allow more thorough heating of the meat than even pints, so should be much safer, not to mention more convenient. It seems that the extension offices are trying to get us to quit canning at home. Hmm. I don't like the sound of that, but have figured it was coming for years now.

Just make sure you process the jars for 90 minutes at the same pressure you would your pints where you live.

Canned venison

I understand canned venison has to be pressure canned because of concern for bacteria. Is it possible to precook the meat entirely and then use the old canning method of water bath canning? Would this be safe?

Norma Overton

No. Sorry, but there are no shortcuts here. Safe is safe, and the only safe home canned meat and vegetables are pressure canned. Deadly bacteria could possibly survive the cooking process and go on to produce spores which are not killed during water bath canning. This shortcut could kill you.

Canning venison

I've never canned meat, so I did a "trial run" this year on a few jars of venison. I followed instructions in my "Blue Book" to brown the meat first and fill the jars with the meat, drippings, and broth. Now I find a thin layer of fat on top of the meat in the jars. Is this fat going to be rancid, and will the fat shorten the length of time the un-

opened jars can be stored? Do you always brown or roast meat before placing it in canning jars?

Judy Madson, Iowa

The thin layer of fat on top of the meat in the jars is perfectly normal and okay. It will not become rancid and it will not shorten the length of time the meat can be stored without losing flavor or wholesomeness.

If I'm in a hurry, as when I must process a whole, large animal, such as a steer, moose, or elk, I will raw pack some of the meat, just to get it put up. But over the years, I have found that the meat that has been browned packs more efficiently, looks better in the jars, and, most important to me, is more tender. Raw packed meat sometimes tends to dry out somewhat as you do not put water or broth on the meat. (If you do, it can expand and force the liquid out of the jar during processing and cause the seal to fail.)

Canning moose and deer

I would like any info on canning moose & deer meat. I am fortunate enough to have a good friend that lives a subsistence life in Alaska. I did can salmon last year and I would like to can a lot of moose meat next year in order to ship it back to Georgia. I really am hesitant to experiment, since my time there will be limited. I need to know how to can the moose properly. I thought I might experiment on deer meat once I have the recipes.

Jimmy Crawford, Georgia

I've canned a whole lot of wild meat: elk, deer, and moose. Basically, you can it up just like you do beef. The times and pressures are the same, which is 75 minutes for pints at 10 pounds pressure and 90 minutes for quarts. I have canned lots of meat raw, but have found that you get more meat in a jar and it ends up more tender if you pre-cook it first. I can up much of my meat as "stew meat," as you can use it in so many different recipes. It can also easily be shredded for such recipes as barbecued beef and fajita meat.

To do this, I use my huge cast iron frying pan on the wood range, and with minimal shortening I begin frying up the first batch of stew meat. While this cooks, I am also slicing slabs of meat and dicing it up in small pieces. Stirring the cooking meat once in a while, until it begins browning, I continue to make piles of stew meat. Once the first pan of meat has cooked, I add water to cover and perhaps some powdered beef soup stock powder.

When the meat has simmered a few minutes, I dump the works in a big pot, add a little fresh grease to the frying pan, and start frying down the next batch. This goes on until the pot holds about all my canner will process in one batch. (My huge old canner will do 9 quarts and 22 pints at one load.)

I reheat the pot of meat until it is all hot, then dip out the meat and pack it into my jars to within an inch of the top, ladling out enough of the broth to just cover it. The jars are then sealed and processed.

While this is going on, I prepare the next batch. Steaks and roasts are done by cutting the meat into pieces half an inch or one inch thick that will slide into wide-mouth jars. These are browned lightly and water and/or broth made with beef stock added as with the stewing meat.

You can raw pack your meat as well, but as I've said, it really isn't faster as you must heat the jars of meat after they are packed, before you process it. And it seems a little more tough than the meat you precook and pack in liquid. But, here's how you do it.

Pack the cold (not frozen) raw meat loosely in wide-mouth jars for roasts and steaks; regular jars for stewing meat. Leave the jars open and place in a pot of hot water so that the boiling water cannot boil up into the jars of meat. Boil this pot until the meat reaches 170°F in the center of the most densely packed jar. Then add a tsp. of salt to the quarts and a ½ tsp. to the pints and seal the jars. Do *not* add liquid. Process quarts for 90 minutes and pints for 75 minutes. This method is not advised by experts because folks have "cheated" and not used a thermometer and processed raw meat that was not hot enough, ending up with bad food.

I *do* question you saying you will ship this meat to yourself in Georgia. I have shipped home canned food several times, only to have rough handling of the boxes open the seals on jars of pickles and chili (some jars even broke). Would it be safer for you to sharp freeze large chunks of boneless meat and pack them in a large cooler with dry ice, all in a heavy plastic bag, tape the cooler shut with duct tape and mail that home, instead? Many sportsmen do this, with excellent results. And it's a whole lot harder to break a cooler than it is a jar.

I also hope you've checked on game rules, as you don't want to break laws regarding game meat shipping.

Using home canned meats

One question, after reading about your canning pork loin and other meats found on sale, can you tell me a few ways you might use your canned meat for meals? We seem to mostly eat meat grilled, baked, fried, or sautéed and I am not sure how meat packed in liquid will work for us. What else can I do with it other than just serving as meat with gravy over potatoes, noodles etc.?

Judith Enke, Missouri

Tonight I boiled fresh garden vegetables: cabbage, onions, potatoes, and carrots. When they were tender, I drained them and poured the broth from a pint of pork loin on them and brought that to a simmer, covered. Then I added 2 Tbsp. of olive oil to a frying pan, added the pork, and gently sautéed that. When it was hot, I added 2 Tbsp. sweet Italian salad dressing and finished stirring the mix until it was beautifully glazed. Quick, easy, and all from the homestead.

I often roast canned meats with vegetables, adding the meat when the vegetables are about halfway tender and spreading barbecue sauce, jam (plum or cherry is great), or a "cookable" salad dressing on first.

Or I pull the meat apart and add barbecue sauce for a great barbecue sandwich, using homemade buns.

Or I dice up the canned meat carefully (if it isn't already) and add to a stir fry … sometimes with a Chinese-type glaze (orange, lemon, sesame, or whatever I feel like) and serve with fried rice, made with the broth from the meat.

Or I'll add the meat to vegetables and gravy or tomato sauce and make a great, hearty stew. As you can see, the possibilities are endless.

Meals

Don't use TVPs when canning spaghetti sauce

I make a vegetarian spaghetti sauce using the usual ingredients (tomatoes, onions, peppers, mushrooms, olives), as well as textured vegetable protein (TVP). I'd like to start canning the sauce, but can't find any information on the processing time for TVP. Any ideas?

Debra Ricketts

If I was canning your vegetarian spaghetti sauce I would can it without the TVP, then briefly add the product as you heat the sauce to use it in your batch of spaghetti. The reason for this is not the length of time you would process the TVP (the same as mushrooms) but the fact that the TVPs will get mushy and dissolve during processing. One of the reasons we use the TVPs is for the texture, which resem-

67

bles meat products. Of course, the other obvious reason is for the flavor. Sausage flavored TVPs are very good in spaghetti sauce as well as in omelets, casseroles, and on pizzas.

Remember to pressure can your spaghetti sauce when using mushrooms, green peppers, meat, or large amounts of TVPs (other than a pinch or two), as they contain soy protein. All of these ingredients are low-acid foods and the acid in the tomato sauce or paste may not be enough to protect the food against dangerous bacteria that would not be killed during a simple water bath processing.

Canned pasta

I just bought myself a new pressure canner and was wondering if you have ever canned macaroni products (goulash, spaghetti)?

I thought I could save myself some money by doing it myself. Chef Boyardee doesn't need the money as much as I do.

Debbie Taylor

Sure, I can several pasta recipes. They're easy, but I can't say we really love canned spaghetti; fresh is so much better. But homemade canned is much better than store-bought. We can't even eat that stuff.

Simply make your favorite recipe, cooking the pasta until just barely done; it needs to expand a bit, but not get tender or you'll end up with mush. As soon as the recipe is done, dip it out into clean quart jars (wide-mouth work best), up to 1 inch from the top. Wipe the rims with a clean cloth, place hot previously boiled lids in place, and screw rings down firmly. Process for the longest time needed for any ingredient, usually the meat. Check in your canning book before starting and jot down the time needed. Go a little easy on the spices, as they tend to intensify during canning and storage. You can always add more when you simmer to heat back up before eating. (As with any other canned food, you should simmer for 15 minutes before tasting to be absolutely sure you kill any possible harmful bacteria.)

Canning fresh noodles

Can you can with fresh noodles such as tortellinis? If so how? Anything you have might help. Thank you.

Tiffany Steveson, Colorado

Yes, you can home can recipes with fresh noodles. I just make sure they are dried fairly well before I can a recipe using them. Then make the rest of the recipe up and just before you put it into the jars, add the noodles. This way, the noodles don't turn to mush in the processing. If you go ahead and completely cook your recipe before packing it into jars, the additional cooking which happens during the processing makes the noodles fall apart and become unappetizing.

I have had great luck in home canning pasta dishes and they are certainly *much* better than the Chef Boy-you-know-who stuff in the stores!

Canning homemade noodles

I have a simple way of making noodles with simply eggs and flour ... they come out thick like dumplings! My problem is my new pressure cooker canning guide says not to can anything with flour in it. It says flour makes steriliza-

tion difficult. Why is this? I have bought chicken noodle soup in the store. Any information or insight would be greatly appreciated.

George Heintz

Every day I hear of things I've done for years ... and even my Grandma did successfully for years, that "you can't do." I know companies are trying to be extra safe and keep people from harming themselves, but that's a new one for me.

I can egg noodles in chicken broth, with pieces of chicken, quite often. They are also good with beef and carrots. I especially like them, as you have "instant" meals that actually taste good.

Make your favorite chicken (or beef) soup recipe, then add dried noodles to hot mixture. Simmer just until limp. Pack into clean, hot quart jars. Wipe rims and seal. Process 75 minutes at 10 pounds pressure. Adjust pressure, if needed, for altitude.

My grandmother canned stewed tomatoes with macaroni for my grandpa. It was his absolute favorite meal.

Canning with noodles

I have an excess of eggs and chicken right now. I could just can the chicken and dry the noodles, but what is the way to can it together ... cook noodles first, or put in jar and let the pressure canning do the cooking?

Caroline Graham

Make your chicken soup, then add one or two handfuls of dry noodles to each quart jar. If you cook the noodles first, you'll end up with mush instead of chicken and noodle soup. Be a little careful when adding your favorite spices to the soup. Salt is fine, but be light in adding the others as canning intensifies the taste of spices. You might want to add more on reheating, before you eat it.

Canning soups

My wife and I have recently made the decision to pursue a more self-reliant form of daily living, as we both are subscribers to BHM. Do you have or know where we could obtain an absolutely foolproof recipe for canning soups? We basically are looking for pressures and boiling times. As you know, there are so many recipes out there that we have gotten quite confused reading these.

Troy and Michelle Hammond, Michigan

I sympathize with your effort, and I know how challenging home canning seems at first. Remember, one rule when canning soups and stews: process the food according to the individual food in the recipe that requires the longest processing time. This is usually meat, which requires 90 minutes at 10 pounds of pressure (adjust your pounds of pressure according to altitude above 1,000 feet above sea level or greater; see your canning book). By reading your canning book, just check your meat, then all of your vegetables. Of vegetables, corn and cabbage take the longest processing of most soup/stew vegetables.

Pressure canning stock

I just got through making 30 quarts of vegetable stock that I use as a green supplement. It's made from kale, carrots, garlic, onions, celery, seaweed, and pure water.

I combine ½ cup vegetable stock with ½ cup chicken stock and drink daily. It really helps with bone aches, arthritis, and muscular aches. When I combine it with the chicken stock it's like taking a one a day vitamin. It energizes me for the day. And no more bone aches for this gal.

To preserve the stock I either freeze it or pour the boiling stock into quart jars and seal, then I store the quarts of stock in the fridge until needed. But it takes up a lot of space in my refrigerator.

Would it destroy a lot of the useful nutrients if I chose to pressure cook my vegetable stocks? I've always heard bad things about pressure canning and how destructive pressure canning can be. Is this true? Do I need to pressure can my stock or just give it a hot water bath?

I would like to have my refrigerator space back.

Cesca

If I felt that pressure canning was destructive in any way, I wouldn't spend so much time and energy doing it. When you use fresh ingredients and follow the directions for the time and pressure, you retain most of the nutrients available.

No, you cannot water bath process any vegetable or meat product. These are low-acid foods and to do so is very dangerous. I realize many people have done and will continue to do this, but it is still dangerous. I would try pressure canning a few jars of your stock and see if you like the results.

Potato soup

Can you home can potato soup?

Judy Green

Yes, you can home can cream of potato soup, but if you use milk or cream in the soup, the end result will look curdled on opening. I much prefer to can small chunks of potato, then I make my own potato soup. This will only take ten minutes, which is about the time it takes to heat a can of cream of potato soup, anyway. Here's my recipe, if you'd like to give it a try. You can also use diced, cooked potatoes instead of canned potatoes.

Jackie's fabulous potato soup:

> 2 Tbsp. margarine
>
> 2 Tbsp. flour
>
> 2 cups milk
>
> 2 Tbsp. chicken soup base (dry)
>
> 1 pint diced, canned, or cooked potatoes, drained
>
> 1 tsp. dehydrated onion
>
> ¼ cup dehydrated, frozen, or fresh peas
>
> ½ cup cheese powder

Melt the margarine in large saucepan, stir in the flour. Add milk and chicken soup base. Stir well. Add potatoes and mash some a bit; leave most chunky. Add the onion and peas if dehydrated. Simmer gently for a few minutes. Then add cheese powder and stir gently, adding fresh or frozen peas. Simmer just a few seconds. If it gets too thick, add milk to correct consistency.

This is a very thick, hearty potato soup that is just great with fresh bread and homemade butter.

Canning turkey soup

I don't own a pressure cooker. Can I can turkey soup and how long should I give it?

Esther Fernandez, Florida

Sorry, but you cannot safely can any low-acid foods, including turkey, soup, vegetables, or meat products, without a pressure canner. The pressure canner raises the temperature of the food above that of boiling water. No matter how long you boil food, the temperature never goes above boiling. This is unsafe for canning low-acid foods as it does not kill bacteria which can cause food poisoning (botulism).

I don't want you to get sick, so try to find a friend or relative that has a good pressure canner that you can borrow. Maybe you can even have them come over for a mini-canning party so they can show you how easy it is to can.

Also, please pick up a good canning book (like my new one!) so you have easy-to-follow directions on canning all your foods.

Milk and canning soup

Can you can potato soup with the milk already added? Thanks,

Merlin

You can home can potato soup with the milk added to it, but I don't think you'll like the results. The milk gives a curdled appearance to the soup which we find unappetizing. It is so easy to just can chunks of potato, then when you're ready to make soup, just make a white sauce using two tablespoons of margarine melted in a saucepan to which you add two tablespoons of flour stirred in to make a paste. Then you should slowly add milk until you get a thickness to the sauce that you like. Finally, add a quart jar of drained potatoes for a nice pot of potato soup.

Canning Brunswick stew — is it safe to do or not?

I read your article about your canning experience and wondered if you have ever canned Brunswick stew. The extension office says you cannot can this stew due to the ingredients. My Brunswick stew has chicken, pork, and beef. The veggies are potatoes, lima beans, tomatoes, onions, white corn, and creamed white corn. The remaining ingredients are Worchestershire sauce, liquid smoke, chicken broth, BBQ sauce, hot sauce, and spices. For years I've been freezing this stew and I'm not happy with the taste and texture of the veggies after freezing. All the ingredients are precooked before adding to the big pot to simmer together for 6-8 hours.

So I wondered if you have ever canned Brunswick stew or any other stew with three different meats, several different vegetables, and seasonings? If you have any suggestions, please share with me.

Pokahontas

Yes, I have canned Brunswick stew and many different mixed stews and other things with mixed ingredients. As I am no "expert" with initials behind my name, I will not advise you to do as I do (and the many years of *Ball Blue Book* canning manuals in years past) which is to simply process the recipe for the length of time required for the ingredient requiring the longest time. Usually this is meat at 90 minutes. All mixed stews and soups must be pressure canned. You cannot water bath can anything with meat or

75

vegetables in the recipe, with the exception of predominantly high-acid recipes, such as pickles or salsa.

I guess some folks couldn't follow directions or somehow goofed up. You'll notice that there are fewer and fewer recipes for honest-to-goodness canning in modern canning manuals because the companies don't want to be sued by someone who simply made a mistake. In a sue-happy world, you can understand this. But it doesn't mean that we must quit canning.

Canning vegetable soup

My question is about canning vegetable soup. I made vegetable soup and used tomatoes that were already canned. I would like to can the soup. Can the tomatoes be recanned if I can the soup?

Dede Haiar

Sure, go ahead and can that soup. I've used pre-canned ingredients a lot. In fact, I can a lot of mixtures during the winter, using tomato products, vegetables, and meats that I quickly canned during the busy harvest season. I'm sure that there is some loss of nutrients, but I'll bet we more than make up for it by canning fresh fruits and vegetables. When I can vegetable soup, I just heat it to boiling, but do not boil. That way, the vegetables do not turn to mush during processing. Good luck and good eating.

Canning cream of mushroom soup

I know you get lots of letters so let me just say I'm a big fan of your articles ... it is because of you I found Backwoods Home Magazine.

That said, so many recipes call for cream of mushroom soup. Do you have a recipe for cream of mushroom soup (using store-bought mushrooms)? And if you do, how would you can it?

Bonnie Summerlin, Oklahoma

I have never been happy with the results of home canned recipes for cream of anything soup; the flour and milk kind of curdle together and won't whip smooth. Instead, I can my mushrooms and chopped mushrooms, then make my soup when I'm ready. The whole thing takes about five minutes.

You can take 2 Tbsp. margarine or butter and slowly melt it with 2 Tbsp. flour, stirring in a medium saucepan. When it is well mixed, begin stirring in whole milk until it thickens nicely. I often add 1 Tbsp. of powdered chicken soup base. Then, I drain and add my home canned mushrooms and barely simmer for 10 minutes; don't boil. It's that easy. If you use dehydrated milk, you can use the mushroom "water" to add to the milk for even more flavor. If you like smaller pieces, whip the mushrooms lightly in your blender or grind them through a meat grinder. The smaller pieces seem to give more mushroom flavor to the soup. You can also add a little chopped chicken or other meat to your soup to give it a heartier taste.

Canning black bean soup

I have searched the web for recipes for black bean soup and how to can it. While finding delicious recipes was

*easy, I have yet to find any ideas on how to can this tasty
soup. Could you please give me some guidance on this?*

Patricia Pittner

Stir up the ingredients of your soup. Boil for 30 minutes.
Ladle hot soup into hot jars to within an inch of the top
of the jar. Remove any air bubbles. Process quarts for 90
minutes at 10 pounds pressure unless you live at an altitude above 1,000 feet, then consult your canning manual
for instructions on increasing your pressure to match your
altitude.

Stuffed pepper soup

*I have the following recipe and I was wondering what
the pressure and time would be to can it. And could I add
more ground beef to it?*

Stuffed pepper soup:

> 1½ cups green pepper, chopped
>
> ½ cup red pepper, chopped
>
> 1 cup onion, chopped
>
> ½ lb. hamburger (optional)
>
> 1 can (14 oz.) diced tomatoes
>
> ¼ cup brown rice, uncooked (can use left-
> over rice)
>
> 2 beef bouillon cubes + 2 cups water (can
> use homemade or canned beef broth)
>
> 2 Tbsp. brown sugar
>
> salt and pepper to taste

Teresa Roh, Pennsylvania

Yes, you can add more ground beef to it, but I'd back off just a bit on the brown rice, as it will swell during processing. You want a light, "soupy" soup, not a very dense end product, for processing safety. You should process this soup for 75 minutes for pints and 90 minutes for quarts, at 10 pounds pressure. If you live at an altitude above 1,000 feet, consult your canning book for directions on increasing your pressure to suit your altitude, if necessary.

Canning thick stew

How thick is too thick (for safety) when it comes to home canning? My hubby isn't much for stews unless they have a good thick gravy, and I'm trying to can up some things that he can simply pour in a pot and heat up himself.

Tracey Roberts, Oregon

It's not safe to can up soups and stews that are fairly thick. If you can pour your soup out in a stream, it's fine, but if it goes "plop, plop," that's way too thick. Some soups and stews that contain rice or noodles will thicken after processing, and are safe, but ones thickened with flour before canning are a little dicey. Teach your hubby to just mix a little flour with a little of the soup/stew broth to make a paste, then pour the rest in with it. As it heats, it will thicken and he'll have thicker stew without lots of extra work.

Canned kale soup

Jackie, here is my recipe for kale soup. If you try it, I'm sure you and your family will love it. In the meantime, can you tell me how to can it?

Kale soup:

> pork bones to make stock (optional)
> 3 quarts water (or other stock — vegetable
>   stocks go great in this)
> 2 lbs. chourico, sliced into ½ inch pieces
>   (other types of sausage, such as linguisa,
>   kielbasa, etc, work too, but I like chou-
>   rico best)
> 1 large red onion, chopped
> 6-8 medium red potatoes, unpeeled, and cut
>   into 1-1½ inch cubes
> ¼ cup parsley, chopped
> 8 cloves garlic
> 1½-2 lbs. kale, stems and all, cut into
>   manageable bite-size pieces — use the
>   real curly type of kale, not decorative. (1
>   bunch of kale is about ½ lb.)
> 2 cans (15 oz.) kidney beans, drained
> 2 cans (15 oz.) diced tomatoes, with the
>   liquid
> 2 bay leaves
> 1 tsp. Italian seasoning
> 1 tsp. red pepper flakes
> fresh ground black pepper, to taste (I start
>   out with about ½ tsp.)

Put pork bones in the water and simmer for about an hour. Remove and discard the bones and add more water to the stock to make three quarts of liquid. (If you don't make the stock, just start with the 3 quarts water or other stock.) Add all the other ingredients to the stock (or water) and bring to a boil. Turn the heat down to a slow boil until the potatoes and kale stems are tender, about 25-30 minutes.

❖   ❖   ❖   ❖   ❖   ❖   ❖

This is one of those soups that, if it's possible, should be made a day ahead and, when it's done, put into the refrigerator overnight and served reheated the next day, as all of the flavors will have married by then.

John Silveira, Oregon

I'll tell you how to can it. And I'll bet you'll like it as well as day-old, as the flavors will really blend well during storage, after processing.

First, make your stock, as usual. Remove the bones and then add all ingredients but the potatoes and kale. Simmer briefly, then add the kale. Simmer again, just until the kale is limp — no longer. Add the potatoes and mix. Dip out the soup, being careful to get a good mix of ingredients in each jar, and fill quart jars to within 1 inch of the top. Wipe the rim with a damp cloth. Place previously boiled new lids on jars and screw rings down on them tightly, but without undue force. Place jars in warmed canner. (The canner will have an inch of water under the inner basket.)

Tighten the lid, leaving the exhaust petcocks open. Turn on heat and wait until steam has exhausted well. The steam should exit the petcocks in a strong, vigorous, steady stream, not little spurts. When this is happening, shut petcocks and wait for the pressure to build up.

As you are relatively close to sea level, you will be processing your soup at 10 pounds pressure. And you will hold it at 10 pounds for 90 minutes. (Remember to adjust the pressure accordingly, should you can this soup above 1,000 ft. altitude above sea level.)

After 90 minutes, turn off heat and allow pressure to return to zero. Then, carefully open the petcocks to release any remaining steam. Open the canner lid, letting the steam rise away from your face. Then remove the jars with a jar lifter and place on a dry, folded towel to cool out of any drafts. When they are cool, you may wash them in warm, soapy water and remove the rings. Your kale soup is ready to store until you need it some wintry day.

Water gone from canned chicken noodle soup

I recently canned some chicken noodle soup. When the time was up on the canning time, I let the canner cool, took the gauge off and then took off the lid. The water was out of the jars, or at least half of it was gone. What is the problem? Is it still good to eat?

Kathy

There are several things that exhaust the fluid from canned goods during processing. The one that usually gets me is getting distracted and letting the pressure get too high, then lowering it to get back on track. A sudden lowering of pressure (as when someone "helps" the pressure canner get down to zero by bumping the petcock or weight) also is a common cause of this.

Because you were canning chicken noodle soup, I'd also be a bit suspicious of the noodles expanding a bit, causing the jars to be too full of food. Jars that are too full of food or filled too high with liquid often cause fluid loss, such as yours.

The food is still good to eat, as long as the seals remain good; they should be indented firmly in the center, with no give whatsoever.

This is a once-in-a-while problem that most home canners run into, sooner or later. Don't let it discourage you, but can on.

Canning meaty chili

I read your article on canning. I have never canned but I want to. My chili has meat products in it. How do I can that? And congrats on your new place; looks like a lot of hard work and great fun. Wish I was there!

Dallas

First, pick up a recent canning manual or book from your county agent, library, or book seller. Basically, you'll make a big batch of your favorite chili, then ladle it hot into clean quart jars, allowing an inch of headspace, seal, and process for 90 minutes in a pressure canner at 10 pounds of pressure (adjusting the pressure upward to suit higher altitudes above 1,000 ft.). Follow the directions for a "meat product" and you'll do great. One warning, though, once you start canning it's addicting. You'll love it.

Canning chili

My boyfriend loves to cook chili and wants to can it him-self. I know we need a pressure canner for that. I want to know if he can use his own recipe of beef, pork, veal, hot and sweet sausage, and the usual ingredients without any problems. How long should it keep? Do you have any suggestions on a good pressure canner and how long we process it for? We have only canned dill pickles in a water bath.

Jane Lippincott, Pennsylvania

Yes, he can use any recipe he loves! You will be canning quarts at 10 pounds pressure (unless you live at an altitude above 1,000 feet and must increase your pressure to suit your altitude, if necessary; consult a good canning manual for directions) for 90 minutes and pints for 75 minutes. It will keep perfectly good for years and years, provided it was properly canned and stored in a dry, reasonably cool (as in the house) area. Any medium/large modern canner will work well for you; avoid the small (cheaper) "pressure cookers." They just won't do the job.

Once you venture into the exciting world of home canning, you'll be hooked. There is no end to the terrific meals you can make with your home canned foods.

Canning homemade chili

I'm interested in canning my homemade chili. What are the rules to follow and do I need a pressure canner?

Alice Taggart

Home canned chili is great. My oldest son, Bill, always asks for my special "Muley chili," which is a spicy chili using mule deer venison. And chili is easy to can. You simply make up your favorite recipe in a big batch, ladle it into hot, clean quart jars to within one inch of the top, wipe the rim clean, and place a hot, previously boiled lid on. Screw down the ring firmly tight and place in a pressure canner and process for 90 minutes at 10 pounds pressure.

Adjust pressure to altitudes, if necessary. Check your canning manual for instructions regarding this.

Canning chili with beans

I was wondering if I am able to pressure can chili with beans. I am only able to find recipes without beans.

Stephanie Faulks, New York

Yes, you may home can chili with beans. I do it nearly every year, which gives us convenient, instant meals without the chemicals included in store-bought chili. Besides, mine tastes like chili, not some flavorless goopy paste.

Make up a big batch of your favorite chili, then ladle the hot chili into quart jars to within an inch of the top of the jar. Remove any air bubbles with a wooden spoon or spatula.

Process the chili in a pressure canner only, at 10 pounds pressure for 90 minutes. If you live at an altitude above 1,000 feet, consult your canning manual for instructions on increasing the pressure to correspond with your altitude.

Canning baked beans and chili

How do you can baked beans and chili? Any particular recipe?

James Coffey, Maryland

Baked beans and chili are among our family's favorites, especially in the winter when the jars are handy to open and heat, giving a quick (15 minute) homemade-tasting meal for hungry sledders or woodchoppers.

You may use any recipe you like, but you must process the jars according to the ingredient which requires the longest processing time in the pressure canner. (You also must use the pressure canner for these low-acid foods or risk food poisoning.)

In both recipes that follow, the ingredient which will require the longest time is beans, requiring 1 hour and 20 minutes for pints and 1 hour and 35 minutes for quarts at 10 pounds of pressure (or higher, depending on your altitude; check your canning book, as you must use the correct pressure for sure seals and food safety).

Baked beans:

> 1 quart dried navy or other small beans (about 2 lbs.)
>
> 2 tsp. salt (to precook the beans)
>
> ½ lb. pork (side pork, ham, or bacon, cut in small pieces)
>
> 3 small onions, chopped
>
> ⅔ cup brown sugar, packed
>
> 2 tsp. salt (for the finished product)
>
> 2 tsp. dry mustard
>
> ⅔ cup molasses

Rinse and pick over the beans, then soak them in 3 quarts of water overnight. Add 2 tsp. salt to beans in soaking water and bring to boil. Cover and simmer 'til skins begin to crack. Drain, saving liquid. Pour beans into a baking dish or bean pot. Add pork and onions. If for religious or other reasons you do not choose to use pork, you can substitute smoked venison or turkey pieces. Combine remaining ingredients. Add 4 cups bean liquid, adding more water if necessary to make the 4 cups. Stir, cover, and bake at 350°F for 3½ hours. Add water towards the end to keep beans a bit "soupy." Pack into hot jars, leaving 1 inch headroom. Keep the beans hot while putting into jars, and work quickly to get them into the canner. Wipe the jar rims. Put boiled lids on and tighten rings firmly, but without force. Process pints 1 hour and 20 minutes, quarts 1 hour and 35 minutes, at 10 pounds (adjust for higher altitudes).

Buying canned bacon

I am trying to locate where to buy canned bacon. About 20 years ago I could buy it by the case at K-mart. I do not remember the name brand; it was from Norway or Denmark. I contacted all of the major canned food producers, no luck. I was wondering if you know of any companies, or have any idea where I could go to buy canned bacon.

Pete Gibson, Arizona

I have had other readers looking for canned bacon, too. And I've had no luck in finding any, anywhere. Any readers out there have a *current* supply for this tasty food?

Canning pork and beans

Do you can pork & beans like you can buy Campbell's Pork & Beans? If so, do you have a recipe you care to share?

Otho Laurance, Oregon

Sure do — every year! Here's my recipe from *Growing and Canning Your Own Food*, my new book.

Beans with tomato sauce and bacon:

> 2 lbs. dried beans
> 1 cup chopped onion
> 3 Tbsp. brown sugar
> 2 tsp. salt
> ¼ tsp. cloves
> ¼ tsp. allspice
> 1 quart tomato juice
> ¼ lb. lean bacon

Cover beans with cold water and let stand overnight. Drain. Cover beans with boiling water by at least 2 inches in a large pot. Boil 3 minutes. Remove from heat. Combine onion, brown sugar, salt, spices, and tomato juice. Bring to a boil. Drain beans. Pack 1 cup beans into pint jars, 2 cups to quarts. Place a nice piece of bacon on top and ladle hot tomato sauce over beans, leaving 1 inch of headspace. Remove air bubbles. Wipe rim of jar clean; place hot, previously simmered lid on jar and screw down ring firmly tight. Process pints for 65 minutes and quarts for 75 minutes at 10 pounds pressure in a pressure canner. If you live at an altitude above 1,000 feet, consult your canning book for directions on increasing your pressure to suit your altitude, if necessary. You can add more brown sugar if you like a sweeter bean or add a little molasses if you want a more "baked bean" taste.

Canning recipes

I have been canning fruits and vegetables for about three years now and I would really love to try to can up some quick meals. I am wondering if regular recipes can be converted to home canning, specifically, this recipe for baked beans. I would like to use dried beans; would I have to use fresh tomatoes or could I use canned? Also, the cola is something I'm unsure about. I'm sure it would cook down before the jarring process, but I really don't know. I would really appreciate any feedback at all, whether general info or specific to this recipe.

Cola baked beans:

> 6 slices thick-cut bacon
>
> 1 large onion, diced
>
> 1 clove garlic, minced
>
> 2 cans (15-oz.) cannellini beans, 1 can drained and rinsed, 1 can undrained
>
> 2 cans (15-oz.) red kidney beans, drained and rinsed
>
> ¼ cup packed dark brown sugar
>
> ⅓ cup molasses
>
> ¾ cup cola
>
> 1 can (14.5-oz.) chopped tomatoes, drained
>
> 2 tsp. dry mustard

Preheat oven to 375°F. In a large ovenproof skillet, cook bacon over medium-high heat until crisp and golden. Drain bacon on paper towels. When bacon is cool enough to handle, crumble and set aside. Pour off all but 1 Tbsp. bacon fat from skillet.

Add onion and garlic to skillet and cook, stirring, until onion is golden, about 5 minutes. Add cannellini and kidney beans, brown sugar, molasses, cola, tomatoes, dry mustard, and crumbled bacon and stir to combine.

Cover skillet, transfer to oven and bake until mixture is bubbly and juices have thickened slightly, about one hour. Serve hot.

❧   ❧   ❧   ❧   ❧   ❧   ❧

Angela Brown, Ohio

Yes, you can home can your recipe; it doesn't differ greatly from many tested recipes. I would advise using dried beans, soaked to pre-soften them. But you can also use canned beans, as well as canned tomatoes. Don't bake your beans, just mix up the ingredients, then pack hot into hot jars, leaving a generous 1 inch of headspace. Process the jars at 10 pounds pressure for 65 minutes (pints) or 75 minutes (quarts). If you live at an altitude above 1,000 feet, consult your canning book for directions on increasing your pressure to suit your altitude.

Canning tamales

My freezer space is limited right now. I want to make a batch of tamales. The only information I have been able to glean about canning them is that one can use parchment paper to wrap them. Do you have any canning tips for me on how to process them? Would regular corn husks hold up? Will the masa dough cook via the canning process or do they need to be fully cooked before they go into the jars?

Jeannie Livezey, Texas

You can use corn husks to can your tamales; I do. I like the flavor of the corn, which is missing with the parchment. No, you don't have to totally cook the tamales; but it's best to steam them a little so they do hold together while you pack them in the jars. If you hold them against a table knife blade with your finger, you can easily slide them into wide-mouth jars. And yes, they do finish cooking while canning. Be sure to process your tamales at 10 pounds pressure for 75 minutes (pints) or 90 minutes (quarts), as they are a meat product. If you live at an altitude above 1,000 feet, consult your canning book for instructions on increasing your pressure to suit your altitude.

Vegetables

Canning garden vegetables

Is there a safe way to can garden vegetables without a pressure cooker?

Virginia Cawthon

No. The only safe way to home can vegetables, meat, seafood, and poultry, which are low-acid foods, is with a pressure canner. The only way you can home can vegetables without a pressure canner is to pickle them, which, using the right recipe, effectively makes them high-acid vegetables because of the vinegar required to pickle them. I make pickled peppers of several types, including an "end of the garden pickle," which uses cauliflower, peppers, carrots, etc. And of course, there is sauerkraut, which is a way to put up cabbage without pressure canning.

Go ahead. Pick up a pressure canner (new on sale, used at a yard sale, or at Goodwill) and start canning all those goodies.

Canning frozen vegetables

My local store has frozen mixed vegetables on sale. I wonder if you could give me directions for canning them? Thanks so much! P.S. I tried your meatball recipe with the cream of mushroom soup and my family loves it!
Sarah Axsom, Louisiana

Glad you liked the meatballs with cream of mushroom soup. We love them too.

To can up frozen vegetables, bring them to a boil in a large pot full of water. Then pack hot in hot jars, leaving 1 inch of headspace. You need to process the mixed vegetables for the length of time necessary for the vegetable with the longest processing time — often corn or potatoes. They can up quite nicely. This also works when your freezer suddenly dies or you have a long power outage that threatens your freezer full of food.

Canning frozen green beans

Can I can frozen green beans? I have lots left over from last year.
Mike Root, South Carolina

Yes, you can, provided that the frozen beans are not freezer burned. Open a container and smell them. Then boil up a small amount and try them. If they taste fine, can away. Be sure to follow normal canning directions. I would suggest heating the beans in boiling water prior to packing them, then packing them hot for best taste and tenderness.

Canning green beans

I know that green beans should be the easiest things to can, but every time I try to can them the water boils out. I leave a one-inch headspace, and I have tried cold pack and hot pack. Is there some secret that I don't know about?

Cathy Barton, Texas

I would seriously take your canner gauge into your local Extension office and have it checked. It sounds like you may be canning at too high a pressure. Another reason that liquid sometimes is sucked out of jars is that the person "tweaks" the pressure relief valves to let steam escape in order to return the pressure to zero. The canner must return to zero by itself, and then … and only then … can you open the petcocks to release any leftover steam. Once this happens, immediately take the jars out of the canner and place them on a dry, folded towel to cool. It messes things up if you leave the processed jars in the canner after processing to cool. Usually the jars seal poorly or not at all.

Trouble canning green beans

I can't believe how much trouble I am having canning green beans. I know it can't be that hard but I can't seem to accomplish it. What am I doing wrong? I snap them into short pieces and put them in cold jars. I put on new lids with rings and put them in a canning kettle with water just up to the rings. I boiled them for at least an hour (last year I tried it without success and assumed it was too short a boiling time). I am getting frustrated because I have done it successfully before.

Mary Stoneberg

I really hate to see folks have trouble home canning. I want everyone to be successful, and I can get you started down the right trail. I can understand why your beans didn't turn out. First, you must can low-acid foods, such as vegetables and meat, with a pressure canner. You cannot safely use a water bath canner for green beans.

A basic how-to for green bean canning goes like this:

Snap your beans into a clean jar. Put your lids into a small saucepan and bring to a boil; remove from heat and keep in water. Put a tea kettle full of water on to boil. Fill quart jars to within 1 inch of the top with green beans and add 1 tsp. of salt, if desired, per quart (half as much salt for pints). Add 2 inches of water to your canner and put on the stove. Fill the jars to within 1 inch of top with the boiling water. Wipe the rims of jars and place the lids in place, screwing rings down firmly tight. Place the jars in the rack inside the canner and tighten the canner's lid down firmly. Exhaust steam for 10 minutes to remove air from the canner. Shut the petcock(s) and let the pressure build to 10 lbs. (or higher, depending on altitude above 1,000 ft.; see your canning manual). When the gauge reads the correct pressure, begin timing and adjust the heat to keep the pressure constant. Maintain this pressure for 20 minutes for pints and 25 for quarts. When the time is up, turn off the heat and let gauge return to zero with no help from you. Then open the petcock to bleed off any remaining steam. Carefully open the canner and, using jar lifters, remove the jars. Place the jars on a dry folded towel to cool. The jars will seal as they cool, ping, ping, ping.

My best advice to all home canners is to buy a canning manual, such as the *Ball Blue Book*, available where canning supplies are sold, and read up before canning each type of food. I've been canning for 30 some years, and haul it out every time ... just in case I've forgotten something.

Canning green beans

For 60 years I have canned green beans like this:
To each quart of beans I add 1 tsp. salt and top it with 1 tsp. vinegar or lemon juice. In water bath I boil quarts for 45 minutes, pints for 30 minutes. Before serving, I boil 5 minutes more. I never, never had spoiled beans and we have never been ill from eating them.

Hanni Goochee, New York

I'm sure your beans are fine, but it is still not safe to water bath any vegetables or meat. The deadly bacteria that causes food poisoning is not present in most food, homes, or jars. Therefore it does not usually affect boiling water bath processed low-acid foods, such as your beans. But it can, and does happen in some instances. It's sort of like pointing a loaded gun at your family. It will probably never go off. But I'd sure not advise doing it! Adding the vinegar or lemon juice is just not enough acid to make them safe.

One exception to this is when you pickle beans or other vegetables. Then, using a lot of vinegar, they become acidic enough to protect them from bacteria which causes food poisoning.

Green beans & potatoes

Have you ever canned green beans and potatoes together and if you have, how is it done? Do I precook the potatoes or can they go in the jar fresh with the green beans?

Will I have to use a pressure cooker or can I do the water bath method and for how long?

Irene Barnes, Illinois

I have never canned potatoes and green beans together. But I have canned green beans, potatoes, carrots, peas, rutabagas, and onions together for a stew base. It's easy to can different vegetables together for use in soups, casseroles, stews, etc. Just process them for the ingredient needing the longest processing time. In this case, you'll be processing your pints for 35 minutes, which is the processing time for cubed potatoes, where green beans' processing time is 25 minutes.

To can your mixture, snap or cut your beans and put into cold, salted water. Then dice up your potatoes and toss into the salted water (which prevents discoloration for a short time). When done, drain and heat in fresh water to boiling, then pack into hot jars to within an inch of the top, filling with the boiling cooking water, leaving an inch of headspace. Process.

Do not use a water bath canner for these or any other vegetable! It is not safe. You must use a pressure canner for all

vegetables, meats, poultry, and fish, as well as any recipes
including them (except pickles).

Canning potatoes

*I have been given a large quantity of new red potatoes.
They are all small in size. I am uncertain as to whether
I have to peel them first before pressure canning. I have
seen directions for peeled and unpeeled. I want your advice on this as I trust what you have to say.*

Kenneth Greene, Georgia

With small potatoes, I usually just scrub them and can
them up. It's easier and we don't mind the very thin peels.
It seems a waste to peel the little guys! And besides, it's
lots of work. I often either scrub or peel and quarter the
larger potatoes. Enjoy your bounty!

Canned potatoes

*Canned some new potatoes. Is it okay if the bottom of the
jars have white sediment on them? Is it from the starch in
the potatoes? Thanks.*

Carol Raup

Yes, this sediment is perfectly natural. It is partly starch
and partly just fine potato particles. If you are making soup
or stew, just dump in the whole jar. Or if this is too much
water in the recipe, pour out some, then use the sediment.
It is also a great ingredient for bread, making the bread rise
better and taste naturally sweeter. Love those home canned
potatoes.

How to can potatoes

We can't wait to try your home canned bologna. But it would be nice to have a recipe for canned potatoes to go with it.

Lanney and Laurie Lavoy, Saskatchewan

I can potatoes almost every year. Mostly because a few jars of them come in handy, from time to time. I can whole, smaller potatoes and those little guys that I just can't throw away at harvest time. The whole tiny potatoes, the size of your thumb, I can scrubbed, with the skins on. When you get ready to use them, you can either use them with the skins on, or simply squeeze them like a grape, and they will pop out, leaving a perfect whole potato.

Potatoes are very simple to can. But I've learned to can them in pint jars, for the reason that if you can them in quart or larger (potatoes only, not stews or mixes), the potatoes will become mushy. They get overcooked, due to the longer time you must process quart or larger jars. Pints can be processed quicker, thus are cooked for a shorter time.

Here's how to can potatoes: wash and sort potatoes, rejecting any with rotten spots, damage, or scars. Peel larger potatoes, cutting into convenient chunks. I leave the smaller ones whole, with the skins on, but scrub them well. Boil for 10 minutes, then pack hot in pint canning jars. Wide-mouth works best. Fill to within one inch of the top, then pour boiling water in to fill within 1 inch of top of jar. Add ½ tsp. salt, if desired. Remove any air bubbles by running a wooden spoon handle down next to the potatoes. Wipe the rim of the jar clean, then place a hot, previously boiled lid on jar and screw down the lid firmly tight. Process pints 35 minutes in a pressure canner. You must use a pressure canner when canning any vegetables or meat.

These potatoes may be used later in potato salad, in stews, soups, potato casseroles, etc. And, because they are already cooked, they make handy, speedy, satisfying meals.

Canning grated potatoes

Do you have any idea whether it would be safe to can grated potato or sweet potato? I know it's not considered safe to can mashed or puréed potatoes or squash, and while even the most conservative sources on safety say pressure canning them chopped is fine, I haven't been able to find anything about whether grating them would be all right (assuming one didn't pack the grated food in too tightly). We freeze a lot of grated sweet potato because we love a quick recipe that uses it that way (cooked up with black beans in a skillet and enjoyed on a tortilla with a little cheese), and if I could can it I could save us the freezer space.

Angela Mazur, Minnesota

I don't think canning either grated potato or sweet potato would be a good idea. First off, it would pack down and make an extremely dense, i.e. not-so-safe product to can. And I'm pretty sure that the end result would be very soft, bordering on mushy. This is one instance where freezing would make you happier.

Canning beets

I would like to can beets without using a pressure canner, as I don't have one and would like to do some beets without pickling them.

Sharon McIntosh, New York

Sorry Sharon, you just can't safely can beets, without pickling them, in a boiling water bath canner. Like green beans (and all vegetables), beets are a low-acid food and must be pressure canned in order to be safe from the deadly botulism toxin. You can pick up a good used pressure canner at many yard sales, flea markets, and so on, complete with manuals in many cases. I have one I bought for $5 at the Salvation Army. It is a good idea to take the canner in to your local extension office to have the pressure gauge tested for accuracy. This is usually a free service.

Canned beets

I am canning beets and I want to know whether it's okay for me to pick and cook the beets one day, then refrigerate them overnight and peel, cut up, and can the beets the next day. I still added the boiling water to cover the beets and pressure canned according to the guidelines, but the directions say to "hot pack" the beets and to go only 2 hours between garden and canner. Does it matter? Hope not, because that is too much work all for one day and besides, those things are too hot to peel right away!!

Kristin Holmes

Yes, you can hold the beets overnight in the fridge. But I would recommend heating them up with a bit of water, covered, until thoroughly heated, then pack into hot jars and fill with boiling water, etc.

Another suggestion is to simply do a small batch of beets every day until done. I've had to scale down this way with my canning, so it's not such a marathon as it often was when I had eight kids at home. When you "plunge beets into cold water," hold them there until they cool down to merely hot but not scalding your fingers. They'll still be hot enough to process and your hands will thank you.

Recipe for canned cabbage

Do you have a recipe for canning cabbage, not sauerkraut?

Emmett Nelson

You bet, Emmett. I can a lot of it. While cabbage will keep a long time in the root cellar or even in a dark corner of a cool basement, there comes a time when it begins to soften and go bad. Before this happens, I can it up and it stays good nearly indefinitely. Cabbage does get a little strong flavored in the jar when canned, but I offset this by dumping out the canning liquid at the time of use, and either boil the canned cabbage in fresh water or milk with a little butter, salt, and pepper. This takes care of things 100 percent.

Canned cabbage:

Choose tight, firm heads. Trim off any wilted leaves, cuts, or bad spots. You can either can your cabbage in chunks, such as quarters, or cut it up as you would for sauerkraut. I prefer the cut cabbage the best. Boil in salted water for five minutes, which wilts it a bit, enabling you to pack more cabbage into each jar. Drain. Pack cabbage into jars to within one inch of the top of the jar. Add 1 teaspoon salt to each quart, or ½ teaspoon to each pint if desired. Fill jar to within 1 inch of top with boiling water. Wipe the rims clean. Place hot, previously boiled lid on each jar and screw down the rings firmly tight. Process quarts 60 minutes and pints 50 minutes in a pressure canner at 10 pounds pressure, adjusting pounds of pressure for altitudes above 1,000 feet above sea level if necessary. See your canning book for more directions.

Canning cabbage

I am trying to find how to can cabbage.

Chris Watts

Cabbage is very easy to can. It does get a bit strong when put up that way, but I just dump out the water in which it was canned and simmer it in fresh water or milk.

To can cabbage, cut it into smaller chunks with the heart removed or slice it. Cover the cabbage with boiling water in a large pot and simmer for three minutes to wilt down the cabbage and make more fit into a jar. Dip the cabbage out and pack into jars, packing tightly. Add a teaspoon full of salt to each quart, if desired. Add hot liquid that the cabbage was boiled in to cover the cabbage to one inch from the top. Process the jars for 30 minutes at 10 pounds of pressure (unless you live at an altitude above 1,000 feet; consult your canning manual for directions).

This cabbage works well in boiled dinners, stews, soups, and other mixed dishes. A favorite way to use it at our house is to drain it well, rinse, then lightly fry in just a little butter. When it is lightly browned, add fresh milk and simmer. It's simple and very good.

Water bath canning cabbage

You discuss canning cabbage. I am new to canning and wonder how long I would need to process the cabbage in a canner that doesn't offer pounds of pressure settings. I just have the big old Wal-Mart blue speckled pot and lid with the metal jar holder inside.

Judi Callahan

Eek! Whoa! Stop! Don't even think about canning cabbage in your blue speckled canner. That's a boiling water bath canner. It's great for high-acid foods, such as fruits, pickles, jams, jellies, and preserves. But low-acid foods, such as vegetables and meats, must be canned in a pressure canner; the one with a gauge or weight indicating pressure in the canner during processing. The pressure canner also has a lock-down lid, needed for the intense steam pressure necessary to kill harmful bacteria, possibly present in low-acid foods.

I know some old-timers still can vegetables and even meat with a water bath canner, using extremely long processing times. But this is not safe. It only takes one bad jar of one food to make your family seriously ill from food poisoning. I look at it like playing Russian roulette; most of the time it's safe … it's the loaded chamber that kills you.

Pick up a good pressure canner. They're not that expensive, and they're usually a once-in-a-lifetime purchase that pays for itself hundreds of times over. There are not many things you buy today that you can say that about, are there?

And once you've bought your canner, here's how I can cabbage:

> Wash well, removing any damaged, loose, or wilted leaves. Cut into pieces as desired, or shred, as for sauerkraut. Boil for five minutes. Pack into jars, to within 1 inch of the top. Add ½ teaspoon of salt to each pint, 1 teaspoon to each quart. Fill to within 1 inch of the top of the jar with boiling cabbage broth. Wipe the rim of jar clean, place a hot, previously boiled lid on the jar, and screw down the ring firmly tight. Process pints 50 minutes and quarts 60 minutes at 10 pounds pressure. (Adjust the pressure to altitude requirements, if necessary. See your canning manual.)

Now that I've told you that you cannot can cabbage in a water bath canner, there are exceptions. How? By making cabbage a high-acid food, instead of a low-acid food, by using vinegar as the acid. Many relishes use cabbage as an ingredient and there is sauerkraut. These, because they are now high-acid due to the vinegar, may be safely canned with your blue speckled water bath canner. Be sure to use a recipe in a canning book or manual to be safe. But I know you meant home canned cabbage, as a vegetable, so we talked about that first.

Processing cabbage

I was reading your recipe for canning cabbage, and I am wondering, you say to process the jars for 60 minutes at

10 pounds of pressure. Now my question is are you using a pressure canner or hot water bath? And do you really mean to process for 60 minutes at 10 lbs. pressure? I'm questioning the 60 minutes.

Rozie Smith, Minnesota

Yes, you must pressure can cabbage, because it is a low-acid food, as are all vegetables (except tomatoes which really aren't a vegetable but a fruit). I have two quite recent canning books which discuss canning cabbage, which isn't USDA recommended because it gets stronger when you can it. One says to process quarts for thirty minutes, and the other 60 minutes. I try to err on the side of safety and I *do* process my cabbage for 60 minutes.

Canning Swiss chard

You mentioned in your last blog that you can Swiss chard — I never knew that could be done or if anyone ever did! I haven't found a recipe for this. We have friends handing us bunches of Swiss chard and I would love to know how to can this so we can enjoy other times of the year. Can this also be done with beet greens? And do these go with water bath or pressure canning? Thanks so much for sharing all your experience with us. You are my "go-to" resource for canning.

Elaine Waskovich, Pennsylvania

Swiss chard and beet greens are great canned. In canning books, most group these under the label "Greens," such as spinach. All are canned the same way in a pressure canner.

Rinse greens thoroughly under running water several times to get rid of grit. Pick off any tough stems or damaged leaves. Place greens in a small amount of water in the bottom of a large pot, covering and heating to steam-wilt. Turn greens when some are wilted to avoid overcooking them. When all are wilted, cut across them several times with a sharp knife to make convenient pieces. Pack hot greens in hot jars, leaving 1 inch of headspace. Add ½ tsp. salt to pint jars, 1 tsp. to quarts, if desired. Pour boiling water over greens, leaving 1 inch of headspace. Wipe rim of jar clean, place hot, previously simmered lid on jar, and screw down ring firmly tight. Process pints for 70 minutes and quarts for 90 minutes at 10 pounds pressure in a pressure canner.

Canning sauerkraut and two cabbage recipes

I LOVE your column. It's the first thing I turn to each month. Thank you for taking the time to share your knowledge and wisdom with everyone, especially us "backwoods wannabes."

My husband and I were fortunate enough to find a lovely home a few minutes south of Seattle. When we bought, we had been dreaming of having our own backwoods home far from civilization, growing our own food ... all the cherished dreams of city folk who want to escape. As it turns out, the universe knew better. We have wonderful "country" neighbors (one is an herbalist & organic gardener with chickens running all over, the other is a basket maker married to a modern-day woodsman). We also have a virgin "back 40" (that's ⁴⁰⁄₁₀₀ of an acre!). We've planted a couple of apple trees and a plum, plowed the rest, and put in six raised veggie beds.

So, after four years here, we're running into something that stumps us:

Sauerkraut: do you have a recipe for making sauerkraut by the pint or quart jar? With just the two of us, we can't eat up even the six cabbages we planted (even after freezing four gallons of borscht) and I can't bear to see them go to waste.

Linda Cunio

As for your abundant cabbage problem: yes, you can make sauerkraut in pint or quart jars, fermenting it right in the jar. It is easy, but does require some monitoring. Here is the recipe:

Sauerkraut, Florida quick method (small amount):

Choose firm, crisp cabbage. Wash and shred finely. One pound of cabbage will pack into a pint jar after shredding. To each pound of cabbage, add 2 teaspoons salt and mix thoroughly. Mix cabbage and salt in a large bowl, 4 to 5 pounds at a time. Pack into pint jars. Place lid on, but do not seal tightly. Air must escape during fermenting. Place full jars in an enamel pan and store in a cool place. Fermentation will be complete in about 10 days. The sauerkraut will be yellowish, with no white areas. It is normal for the jars to leak fluid into the pan, thus the reason for the pan. When fermentation is complete, add enough brine, made up of 2 tablespoons salt to 1 quart of water, to cover the kraut in the jar, leaving about 1 inch of headroom. Wipe the rim of the jar clean with a clean cloth. Place lid, which has been boiled, on the jar and screw down the ring firmly tight. Process jars in a boiling water bath for 30 minutes. Adjust time, if needed, for higher altitudes. Check your canning manual regarding this.

But too much cabbage? That doesn't seem possible, considering all the fantastic ways you can use it! Besides the obvious uses, such as coleslaw, cabbage salad, cabbage rolls, and stir fries, I also love fresh cabbage and pepper relish, which is a refrigerator recipe, and cabbage and beet chutney, which is a spicy canned treat. Here are the recipes, in case you're interested:

Fresh cabbage and pepper relish:

> 1 sweet red pepper
>
> 2 green bell peppers
>
> 1 Tbsp. chopped onions
>
> 2 cups cabbage
>
> ¾ cup vinegar
>
> 2 Tbsp. brown sugar
>
> 1 tsp. salt
>
> 1 tsp. whole mixed pickling spices
>
> 1 clove garlic

Chop peppers and onions. Mix with finely shredded cabbage. In a pan bring vinegar, sugar, and salt to a boil. Add spices and garlic. Cover and cool. Pour through a strainer over vegetables. Stir well. Cover and chill well. I often add, in addition, 1 teaspoon celery seed. This is very good, and only takes minimal work and time.

Cabbage and beet chutney:

> 2 lbs. cabbage (red is pretty)
> ½ lb. onions
> 2 lbs. beets, raw
> 3 oz. salt
> 1 lb. sugar
> 2 oz. peppercorns, in bag
> 2 oz. mustard seed
> 1 quart vinegar

Finely chop the cabbage and onion. Peel and finely dice beets. Put remaining ingredients into a pan, bring to a boil, then add vegetables and simmer until very tender. Remove bag of peppercorns. Put into hot, sterilized jars to within half an inch of the top. Wipe the rim clean. Place hot, previously boiled lid on jar and screw down ring firmly tight. Process in boiling water bath for 10 minutes. This makes about three pints.

Then there's Indian Relish, Three Cups Relish, Cabbage and Beet Relish, Chow Chow for pickle starters, and egg roll filling, milk-fried shredded cabbage, sweet and sour cabbage, New England boiled dinner (uses quartered cabbage), Pasties, and on into the night. Why, I could use up eight cabbages in a week, with just the three of us. Sounds so good, I think I'll go out and whack a couple right now.

Canning broccoli and cabbage

We live off the grid and very soon will no longer have the availability of freezer space. We do a lot of canning, but what we are wondering about is broccoli and cabbage. Can these be canned? All my books say it is not a good idea. I know that cabbage can be canned as kraut, but we like plain old cabbage best. We've tried to root cellar it, but our conditions so far haven't produced a good keep. What can we do to preserve our favorite broccoli?

Greg and Carol Kumher

My goodness, how the canning books have changed. I've seen so much good information replaced with "gourmet" recipes and the like. Yes you can home can cabbage. But it does tend to be a little strong tasting, i.e., pretty cabbagey. It isn't bad, and I usually dump the water it is canned in and heat the cabbage in fresh water. This removes much of the strong taste. In soups, stews, and other mixed dishes, you don't notice it a bit. Our favorite way to use canned cabbage is to drain it, then fry it in 2 tablespoons of butter. Then I add just enough milk to simmer it in and simmer gently for just long enough to nearly dry it up. Pretty darned good!

To can cabbage, I shred it, then boil it just until it wilts. Pack it in quart jars, and fill the jar to within half an inch of the rim with the liquid it was boiled in. Add a teaspoon of salt if you want. Wipe the rim, put on a pre-boiled warm lid, and screw a ring down firmly tight. Then place in your canner and process the quarts for 60 minutes at 10 pounds. (Adjust pounds of pressure, if needed, according to altitude).

Broccoli sucks when canned. It gets strong, mushy, and limp. But broccoli is one of our favorites, too. So instead of canning it, I dry it. Broccoli is very easy to dry and re-

111

constitutes well, too. Simply cut your flowerets, then blanch for 1 minute. Then chop them up, fairly small (1 inch max) and lay out in a single layer on either a cookie sheet to be placed in a shaded hot place (attic, hay loft, stove oven, with only pilot on, etc.) or in a dehydrator. Even though we live off grid, I still use my dehydrator, timing my work with dehydrating foods. I can get a batch pretty well started in the dehydrator, then simply let it finish by itself on the counter, still on the dehydrator trays.

Broccoli is "done" when it feels like wood: crunchy. I store it in miscellaneous glass jars. It keeps forever. Then when I want to add broccoli to a soup, casserole, or other dish, I simply pull out a handful and give it a scrunch and toss it in. It doesn't work too well as a side dish on its own. You must reconstitute it in boiling water for this. I do this the night before and, when the pan with the soaking broccoli is cool, I cover it and put it in the fridge overnight, until needed, then I reheat it.

Crunchy canned cabbage

One more question for you. When I was a youngster I remember my grandmother canning cabbage. The cabbages were cut into wedges and packed in quart jars and a vinegar solution added. This had a crunchy and much milder flavor than sauerkraut. All the canning books I have read say you cannot can cabbage. Have you ever heard of preparing cabbage in this manner?

Cynthia Wiginton, New Mexico

About your question on cabbage, the Amish make a recipe that sounds similar to yours. I haven't made it, but it does sound good. The reason books say you can't can cabbage is that when you can cabbage it does get a little strong tasting. I remedy this by pouring out the liquid when I open a jar and either using the cabbage in a recipe with other liquid or simmering it in milk or fresh water when I heat it up. That effectively reduces the strong taste. Here's the Amish recipe:

Canned cole slaw:

> 1 large head cabbage
>
> 1 tsp. celery seed
>
> grated carrots, if desired
>
> ½ cup chopped onion
>
> 1 tsp. salt
>
> ½ cup vinegar
>
> 2 cups sugar

Cut cabbage and place in a large bowl. Mix other ingredients well and pour over the cabbage. Let set ½ day in a cool place. Pack into sterilized jars. Process for 10 minutes in a water bath canner.

Squash and spaghetti sauce

Hi Jackie ... HELP! I have been searching through all my back issues of BHM *for your recipe for making and canning spaghetti sauce, but still haven't found it. I remember you added summer squash among other veggies, and since our garden has been very prolific this year, I'm trying to get everything possible freezed, canned, or dehydrated.*

113

What is the best way to preserve winter squash? We like it on the dry side like mashed potatoes with butter and a little brown sugar. I've frozen it before but found it soupy. We live in a mobile home on 1.1 acres (in Michigan) without a root cellar to keep veggies through the winter.

Alice

You know, Alice, I don't remember writing a recipe for making spaghetti sauce with summer squash and other veggies in it. I'll tell you this, I incorporate squash in a heck of a lot of recipes that it's not "supposed" to be in, though. What I usually do, regarding spaghetti sauce and squash, is to bake a spaghetti squash, then cut it in half on a cookie sheet. Remove any seeds and fluff up the strings. Then I dump a quart of home canned spaghetti sauce over it, sprinkle liberally with grated mozzarella cheese, and bake until the cheese is lightly tan in spots. That tastes divine.

You can chop up your summer squash and add it to about anything, from pickles to your spaghetti sauce, and no one will be the wiser, as it doesn't have much of a taste until you do something with it. I even slice it thin and add to my cucumber and onions with sour cream.

I can chunks of squash to use if we should run out of fresh squash. I don't have a root cellar either, and simply store my squash under the bed, next to the cold wall and out of the light. To can it this way, just cut up two-inch chunks of raw squash, place it in your wide-mouth canning jar, add a teaspoonful of salt if you want, and cover the squash to within an inch of the top of the jar with boiling water. Then process the jars for 90 minutes at 10 pounds of pressure (unless you live at an altitude above 1,000 feet, then check your canning manual for instructions).

When you use the home canned squash, drain off the water, place in a baking dish in the oven, pat with butter, and sprinkle with brown sugar. Bake until done or as dry as you like. We, too, don't like mushy squash.

Don't forget to use your squash in "pumpkin" pies for the best pies imaginable, in breads, bars, casseroles, and egg nog. Get creative. It's more versatile than most people realize. I dry quite a bit of squash, then grind it to flour and add it to my whole wheat bread. No one ever guesses, and I sure don't tell 'em.

Canning winter squash

I've frozen winter squash and it is, in my opinion, horrible. I've found recipes for canning it but I've read it doesn't taste good either.

Our basement isn't cool enough to keep it and it will get too cold in the garage by February and freeze.

Welcome to Minnesota. I live here too.

Sherry Morse, Minnesota

Thanks for your welcome, Sherry. We are enjoying our new northern Minnesota homestead a bunch. I also hate frozen winter squash. It is great canned, though. Don't believe everything you read. When I serve my own canned squash, I chunk it up and cook it as little as possible. Also, I often bake it, before serving, to dry off some of the liquid and get a consistency my family likes. I do not purée it. That would be yucky, unless you used it in baking. Squash makes a great "pumpkin" pie.

Don't give up on your basement. Get a big cardboard box, put it in the coolest corner of your basement, and stack a few squash in there. Throw an old quilt over the box and check on the temperature. You'll be surprised at how much difference that makes. Any good keeping variety of winter squash should do just fine for several months.

Preserving yellow crook-neck squash for frying

What is the best way to preserve yellow crook-neck squash for frying? Seems that everything we have tried caused them to have a bad taste when cooked.

Gary Williams

To preserve your summer squash for frying, pick the smaller ones with very tiny seeds, for it seems to be the seeds in larger squash that causes off tastes. Slice them up in half-inch thick slices. Pack them into a jar to within an inch of the top, add a teaspoon of salt, if desired, then fill the jar to within an inch of the top with boiling water. Process pints for 30 minutes and quarts for 35 minutes in a pressure canner, at 10 pounds pressure unless you live at an altitude above 1,000 feet. If so, consult your canning manual for pressure adjustment.

Tops of my canned corn are dry. Is it okay to eat?

You have done it now; you have gotten me hooked on canning again after 40 years. I am 83 years old and my kids bought me a pressure canner two years ago, and I was afraid to use it. Once I did, I loved it, and I am canning. One question — I canned corn, and I didn't put enough water in the jars. The top of the jars are dry. Will the corn still be okay to eat? They all sealed nicely. I have received Backwoods Home Magazine *for years and I always read you first.*

Altha Hankins, Arkansas

Congratulations on rejoining the growing ranks of home canners. Isn't it fun? Yes, your corn will be okay to eat. Sometimes, however, corn tends to darken when it is out of the liquid. This looks unappetizing and I just spoon off the dark kernels and those underneath are just fine. Of course, always smell your corn when you open it to make sure that the seal was good and the corn hasn't by some chance spoiled. (This is very rare.)

Corn for seeds and canning

I would like to know a good corn that you can save the seeds yearly for yellow corn on the cob and a white corn for cream corn that can be canned.

Judy Smith, Alabama

I think that the best open pollinated yellow corn is True Gold. It was bred back from a hybrid to a stable, open-pollinated sweet corn that tastes as good as most hybrid sweet corns. One of my favorite white sweet corns is Country Gentleman. It is as sweet as many hybrids, has a large ear, and remains sweet and tender for several days following maturity. It will make very good creamed corn for you.

Brown canned corn

How do you keep your canned corn from turning brown?
Carole-Anne Hopkins, Wyoming

There are several possibilities when canned corn turns brown. The corn could have been too mature and started to get starchy; use corn that is still very milky when you pop a kernel with your thumbnail. It could have been processed at too high a temperature. Have your gauge checked

117

if your canner has one; it may be faulty. The water/juice may not have covered the corn during canning. Keep the pressure steady, because sometimes the liquid blows out of the jar during drops/rises in pressure. A few varieties of corn are suspected of browning during canning. These are usually the super sweet varieties with high sugar. If that's the case, try a different kind next year.

Better luck next time! This is not real common.

Canning corn

This is my first year of growing a garden. The corn turned out exceptionally well. I was just wondering how do you can corn?

Emily Lindstrom, Michigan

Sweet corn is very easy to can. All you need to do is to shuck the corn, pick the silks off it, and slice the corn off the cob. You can buy special cutters to do this. One I use is like a saw blade, bent into a circle on two flexible metal handles you squeeze to tighten the cutting circle on the corn cob. Standing the cob on its big end, you shove the cutter down, while turning it slightly back and forth. The kernels fall right into the pan you have under the cob. I use a big turkey roaster or a large pie pan.

Of course, you can simply slice the kernels off with a sharp knife, too.

Once the corn is off the cob, you can either cold pack it, which simply means packing it cold into clean canning jars to within an inch of the top, adding a tsp. of salt to each jar, then pouring boiling water into the jar to within an inch of the top. It's a good idea to run a plastic or wooden spoon down around the corn to release any air pockets that might have formed.

Corn, being a low-acid food (as are all vegetables but tomatoes), *must* be processed in a pressure canner. You will process pints for 55 minutes and quarts for 90 minutes at 10 pounds pressure unless you live at an altitude over 1,000 feet. In that case, you simply increase the pounds pressure by increments depending on the altitude; see a canning manual for directions.

You can also hot pack corn. This results in a prettier, more even jar of corn; in cold packing, the corn sort of floats to the top of the jar, leaving liquid in the bottom. Same taste; it only looks different.

To hot pack, simply add water to the cut corn in a large kettle. About a cup of water for each quart of corn or a little more is right. Just heat the water and corn to a boil, then scoop out the corn and pack loosely into a clean, warm jar to within an inch of the top. Pour in enough of the water it was boiled in to cover the corn to within an inch of the top of the jar. The processing time is the same.

When the time has been reached, turn off the heat and let the canner cool until the gauge reaches zero. Then release the safety petcocks slowly and open the canner, being careful to open it away from you so that any leftover steam doesn't scald your face or arms. Lift out the jars with a jar lifter and place on a dry, folded towel in a draft-free area to cool. When they are cool (usually overnight), you may remove the rings and wash the jars. Test each jar to make sure the center of the lid is indented tightly. Poke it gently with a finger. There should be no give to the lid; it shouldn't pop down and up. It should remain tightly indented. Dry the jars and store in a cool, dry, dark area.

If you do not have a canning manual, pick up one at any large store or borrow a book from your library until you finish. When you can, you need a canning manual. I've been doing it for over 35 years and wouldn't think of canning without one on the table!

Canning hominy

I would like to know how to lye corn to make hominy and also how to can it. Pressure or water bath?

Glenie Peebles

Here's my grandma's recipe for hominy, made using lye:

Put 2 quarts of dry field corn in a large enameled pan with no chips. Add 8 quarts of water and 2 ounces of lye. Boil vigorously for half an hour. Then steep for 20 minutes with no heat. Rinse off the lye with several hot water rinses, then several cold water rinses. Work hominy well with hands until dark tips of kernels are removed. Separate the tips by floating them off the kernels. Add water to cover hominy by an inch or more. Boil 5 minutes; change water. Repeat 4 times. Then cook until kernels are soft. Drain.

Pack hominy into jars to within 1 inch of the top. Add 1 tsp. salt to each quart jar, ½ tsp. to each pint jar. Fill to within ½ inch of top of jars with water in which corn was cooked or boiling water. Wipe the rims clean, place hot, previously boiled lids on each jar and screw down the rings until they are firmly tight. Process pint jars for 60 minutes and quarts 70 minutes at 10 pounds pressure. (Adjust the pressure to your altitude if necessary; see your canning manual.)

The canning information is current. Never use a water bath canner for any low-acid vegetable or meat product. These are low-acid foods, which are dangerous to can without pressure.

Canning corn & sauerkraut

In your pantry of stored supplies I did not see any canned corn. Do you have a good recipe for canning sweet corn? We have tried and it's not real good.

Judy Smith, Alabama

We do have lots of sweet corn on my pantry shelves. In fact, it's one of our favorite vegetables to can. It comes out so tender and sweet; just like corn on the cob. I also make corn mixtures to add to stews, soups, and casseroles. I have corn and sweet peppers; corn and carrots; corn with peas, onions, and potatoes; and corn, potatoes, carrots, onions, and rutabagas down in my pantry right now. And that's not mentioning corn salsa and corn relish.

When you can corn, you probably don't want to can super-sweet varieties, as the sugar in the corn can often turn brown and make the corn look and sometimes taste unappetizing.

Canning sweet potato butter

I'm looking for a recipe for sweet potato butter. The sweet kind that would be spreadable on muffins, toast, etc. I have found several recipes but none with canning directions. As I would like to put them up, I would like help. Would any recipe I might find that says to pack in canning jars be okay to water bath them, and how long for?

Nancy

I have an old, old sweet potato butter recipe for canning that I have used and I would assume one could use any spice or variation, as long as the sugar to sweet potato ratio remained about the same, since the sugar preserves the low-acid fruit, just as it does for pumpkin butter. Now I can't "recommend" that you can this preserve as it isn't approved or tested by experts. But the ratio of mashed, cooked sweet potatoes to sugar is: for every cup of mashed sweet potatoes add three quarters of a cup of sugar and a pinch of salt and spices (cinnamon, cloves and allspice) to taste. I use brown sugar, but that is a matter of taste. Pack the hot butter in hot, sterilized pint or half-pint jars and process in a boiling water bath for ten minutes, counting from the time the water begins to boil with the jars in it.

Canning eggplant

Can eggplant be home canned? Does it need to be blanched or anything? All the canning references I have are for freezing, and I don't have a lot of freezer space.

Jim Strokotter, Michigan

Yes, Jim, you can home can eggplant, but I'm not sure you'll like the results. Basically, it is canned like you would summer squash or zucchini. And the results are about the same: not so hot. It tends to get mushy and flavorless. One way to beat that is to can slices of eggplant in spaghetti sauce. It still is a bit soft, but much more flavorful than otherwise. Remember, when canning any combination, such as meat and vegetables, or tomato sauce and squash, to process for the longest time for any ingredient. Also, if any ingredient, such as meat or a vegetable, must be pressure canned, you must pressure can the combination.

With the tomato sauce/eggplant mixture, heat tomato sauce to boiling, add slices of eggplant, and simmer five minutes. Dip out eggplant into clean wide-mouth jars. Fill to within one inch of the top, adding tomato sauce to cover to within one inch of the top. Adjust lids. Process in pressure canner for 30 minutes at 10 lbs. pressure (adjusting pressure for altitude, if necessary — see your canning manual).

Canning pumpkin butter

I want to make and can pumpkin butter, but am having problems. I'd charge ahead with my own "recipe," but have safety concerns with the long term preservation aspect of it. The recipes I have found suggest pumpkin butter be made with commercially canned pumpkin purée. I would like to start with a fresh pumpkin. But other recipes I have found state that pumpkin should not be canned. So I'm hesitant to make pumpkin purée, add the sugar and spices, and then hot water bath it. Do you know if that'd be safe? We were wondering if perhaps the commercial canning process does something to kill off bacteria, etc. that we couldn't do so well at home. Or if the pumpkin lacks the natural acidity to kill off things for itself. What about using apple juice?

Ask Jackie

I feel a little stuck between being a child of modern commercially packaged everything and a would be do-it-yourselfer. We currently try to live a simple lifestyle, gearing ourselves up for the day we do it full-time. I've said to my spouse a couple of times that I think it would be fun to spend a few days with you just to take the mystery and awe out of the self-sufficient lifestyle. Let me know if you ever open a guest house or start weekend seminars!

Becky Erickson, Colorado

We never thought much about our lifestyle as having much mystery or awe about it. Some days there's so much to do that we have a hard time convincing our half-century plus bodies to get up in the morning.

The more you live it, the more natural it becomes, I guess.

Okay, to your pumpkin butter. Yes, you can home can pumpkin anything. I can it every year in glass jars. Here I get into trouble; my recipe for pumpkin butter does not require pressure canning. It's from a 1975 Kerr book. To be safe, I suppose you can pressure can your butter as per pumpkin, but I've used the "unsafe" method for a score of years and am still kicking. Here's my recipe, which I am not advising you to use. Spices can be adjusted to preference.

Pumpkin preserves:

> 4 lbs. pumpkin
> 2 lemons
> sugar
> ½ tsp. each cloves, cinnamon, nutmeg
> pinch salt

❧ ❧ ❧ ❧ ❧ ❧ ❧

Mash the pumpkin and lemon meat in preserving kettle. For every cup of pumpkin, add ¾ cup of sugar and a pinch of salt. Add the spices. Mix and let stand overnight, refrigerated. In the morning, boil slowly, stirring well. Pour the mixture into sterilized half-pint jars to within ½ inch of the top. Put on a cap, screw the band firmly tight, and process five minutes in a boiling water bath.

❧ ❧ ❧ ❧ ❧ ❧ ❧

Do not attempt to make pumpkin butter with less sugar if water bathing it, because pumpkin is low acid. Otherwise, it requires pressure canning to be safe from bacteria. In the above recipe, the sugar acts as a preservative. And no, commercially canned pumpkin is in no way better than home canned, nor do they add anything to kill bacteria. To be safest, you probably should pressure can your pumpkin butter for 30 minutes (for pints) at 10 pounds pressure — just in case.

Canning pumpkin

I would like to know why I can't find directions for hot water bath canning of fresh pumpkin. I need to know how long to process quart jars in a hot water canner. Can you help? I do not want to use a pressure canner. I have done this before and had no problems but I forgot how long to process the jars. What is the time table for hot water canning to the time table for the pressure cooker method?

Gloria Broadwater

It is not safe to water bath process pumpkin. I know that lots of people have done it, but to be safe, pumpkin and all other vegetables and all meats, must be home canned in a pressure canner.

Fruits (and tomatoes which are technically a fruit) can be hot water bath canned.

Pressure canning is very easy to do, believe me. It is scarcely more difficult than boiling water in the water bath canner. But if you are dead set against canning pumpkin with a pressure canner, either freeze your puréed pumpkin or dehydrate it in quarter-inch thick slices.

Canned wild mushrooms

In the "Emergency Preparedness and Survival Guide," you have a picture of canned wild mushrooms. I would be pleased with that recipe.

Linda Kindlesparger, Illinois

Canning mushrooms is easy, but the experts now warn not to can wild mushrooms, because some people picked poisonous mushrooms by mistake and canned them up. I don't often listen to "experts" who are trying to keep us safe from ourselves. Of course, every mushroom hunter should only hunt mushrooms they can positively identify. That makes sense. And if you're going to eat 'em, why not can 'em? I do. Frequently.

Be very careful in your picking, but I'm sure I don't have to tell you that. Here's how I can them:

> Sort the mushrooms and soak in salted ice water for 10 minutes to remove any sand or insects. Morels often harbor both of these and are one of the best mushrooms. Can small mushrooms whole, removing any large, tough stems. Larger mushrooms may be sliced.

Place in a pot and cover with water. Boil for 10 minutes. Pack hot into pint or half-pint jars. Add salt (1 teaspoon to pints), if desired. Cover the mushrooms with boiling water to within half an inch of the top of the jar. Wipe rim of jar clean and place hot, previously boiled lid on jar, screwing ring down firmly tight. Pressure can only at 10 pounds pressure (adjusting pressure upward for higher altitude; check your canning manual for directions) for 45 minutes.

I use these wild mushrooms in a lot of recipes, from pizza to stews. They're great.

Canning garlic

I've been looking for a canning recipe for garlic; I want to can it plain. How can it be done?

Virginia

You can home can garlic, although it really is better either kept fresh, raw, in a cool, dry, dark place, or dehydrated. I usually slice peeled whole cloves of garlic in half, then dehydrate until brittle. A quick whir in the blender or hand food chopper turns this dry garlic into granulated dehydrated garlic. It is very good, easy to store and use.

However, if you really want to can it, you can do this by peeling the cloves and either chopping them — to make minced garlic — or using whole cloves.

Simmer the garlic in barely enough water to cover it for 5 minutes. Then pack hot into hot jars to within ½ inch of the top of jar. Add liquid in which garlic was boiled to within ½ inch of the top of jar. Add ½ teaspoon of salt. Wipe the rim clean, place a hot, previously boiled lid on the jar and screw down the ring firmly tight. Process pints for 40 minutes in a pressure canner, at 10 pounds pressure, adjusting the pressure to your altitude if necessary. (See your canning manual for adjusting to your altitude.)

Canning horseradish

I have just made horseradish for the first time and it's hot. They say that to keep your horseradish hot you have to keep it cold. If so, how do you get the vacuum seal if you don't heat it like in canning? The storebought stuff has a vacuum seal and can be hot depending on the brand. Do you know how it is done?

Neal Pomfret, Ontario

I've not had much trouble keeping horseradish hot when processing; it's either good and hot, or it's not. Here's how I put it up. I think you'll like it this way.

Grate your horseradish root finely. Measure the result and measure enough vinegar into a saucepan to equal half the horseradish. Add ½ teaspoon of salt to each cup of vinegar. Have sterilized jars, held hot, and boiled lids ready. You will need your water bath canner full enough to cover your jars, plus 1 inch. This needs to be hot and ready, as well.

Boil your vinegar-salt solution, then add horseradish and bring back to a boil. Dip the horseradish out quickly and fill jars to within ½ inch of the top, wipe the rim, place a lid on, and screw the ring down firmly tight. Place filled jars in a water bath canner and process for 15 minutes at a rolling boil, counting from the time your canner first comes to a full boil.

Dehydrating and canning minced onions

I want to can some minced onions, but I can't find any information on it. I would like to put them up in half-pints. I don't know if they can be raw packed or do I need to cook them?

Cindy Schneider, Florida

Canning minced onions is simple and quick to do, although you may find it even quicker to dehydrate them. I do this, mainly to save time and jars. Just chop your onions as fine as you want, pack them into half-pint canning jars, add ½ tsp. salt if you wish for flavoring, then pour boiling water over them to within ½ inch of the top of the jar. Process for 45 minutes at 10 pounds pressure (unless you live at an altitude higher than 1,000 feet; consult your canning manual for directions).

Dehydrating them is even quicker; just chop them, lay them out in a single layer on a cookie sheet, or, better yet, on a tray in a dehydrator and dry until they are crisp. Stir as needed to dry consistently. After they are dry, store in an airtight jar. I also grind many onions after dehydrating, to make onion powder, which I use almost daily in my cooking. The ones I whiz in my old blender are simply sliced ¼ inch thick in whole slices, dried, then whizzed. Then I dry the powder a bit more to make sure it is absolutely dry, and store it. Half a bushel of onions makes a quart or a little more of onion powder. Talk about storage convenience!

Canning salad dressing

Is it possible to can homemade salad dressing, both ranch and French type? How can we do it? A friend who sells salad greens at a farm market would like to do this. Thank you for your very practical column, especially the steam canner warning!

R.B., Ohio

While I'm sure homemade salad dressing *could* be home canned, I've never found reliable directions for doing so. As soon as I find directions I'll be sure to let readers know.

Canning pesto

Can you home can pesto? I assume that you can, since you can buy it in cans at the store, but I don't know the processing time. I have canned baba ghanooj and so on when overseas, but didn't know if there was a trick with pesto.

Nadine

Anything you find canned in the store can be home canned, but several items, such as pesto, will not be found in your home canning manuals. The only reason I would not recommend canning pesto is that it is so much better made fresh with basils from your own herb bed. Those delicate flavors will not be as perfect if you can it, which of course, must subject it to heat.

But if you want to can it, I'd recommend using half-pint jars; you don't want leftovers.

Using your favorite recipe — typically basil, peeled cloves of garlic, and olive oil, crushed well together — pack it into clean jars to within half an inch of the top.

Wipe the rim, place a previously boiled, warm lid in place, and screw down ring firmly tight. Process at 10 pounds pressure (adjust the pressure upward for higher altitudes; check your canning manual) for 45 minutes.

Discolored canned pesto

I have two questions for you. I have never tried canning before and this year for Christmas I'm thinking of making up baskets with a variety of stuff in them. One of the items will be my homemade pesto which I would like to can, but I am worried that the heat used in canning will discolor and ruin the flavor of the delicate sauce. So is there any way to can pesto without this happening, or any other way to can that does not involve heat?

Stephanie Payne

Pesto is best fresh but I'm sure you could can it, though you'd have to experiment as to retain the flavor and appearance. And to can it you will have to use a pressure canner, i.e., use high heat.

As to your second question, you can use a stock pot or any other large container as a hot water bath canner. My grandmother used to use her copper boiler to can peaches and other fruits in. You do need to keep the jars off the bottom of the container or they will break. A wire rack works great. You have to have a big enough container or pot to allow the water to maintain a rolling boil an inch or more over the jars, and a top is necessary to quickly bring the water to a rolling boil, and keep it there for processing.

All low-acid foods, such as vegetables, meat and poultry, and any mixes (soups, stews, etc.) must be pressure canned using a pressure canner, not a pressure cooker, which is not large enough, nor intended for canning.

Tomatoes

Canning fresh pack tomatoes

I tried canning fresh pack tomatoes for the first time. I followed the directions exactly, but when I took them out of the canner, the fruit was at the top of the jar and the liquid was all at the bottom. Is this normal? I want to make sure that I did not do something wrong.

Karen

When you cold pack tomatoes or other fruit, it floats to the top of the jar. This is why home canners who vie for prizes at fairs always hot pack tomatoes and other fruit; it stays evenly distributed in the juice in the jar. It is "prettier." I often cold pack tomatoes when I'm in a hurry, but I usually mash them in tightly. When they're left to their

133

own space, too much juice floats them badly. They're still great to eat, just have more juice than "meat."

Floating tomatoes

Help! I have just finished canning my first bunch of tomatoes of 2000. I pack the jars tightly, at least I think I do, get the air bubbles out, add salt and lemon juice, process them in a hot water bath 45 minutes for quarts, right? The USDA says 85 minutes. Which is correct? But after I remove them from the kettle, the liquid and tomatoes have separated and on some jars, the liquid is down 3 inches. What am I doing wrong?

Cindy

For your "floating tomatoes," see the reply to "Canning fresh pack tomatoes."

And about the juice, which has boiled out: it could have been that the tomatoes were a little too fully packed in the jars or that water did not entirely cover the jars while processing. Check for both, next time. Also, hot packing tomatoes results in less of this. At any rate, the tomatoes are perfectly okay to eat, providing the jars are sealed.

I process my quarts of tomatoes for 45 minutes in a hot water bath.

Awful-tasting green tomatoes

I just opened a jar of canned green tomatoes I canned last November and they tasted awful although the color was good, the brine was clear, and they are crisp. Tomatoes are hard to grow here in Phoenix, Arizona, because of our very hot summers. These tomatoes were growing and putting on fruit from the middle of September to De-

cember. I picked them around Thanksgiving and canned them immediately. As I said, they looked good but not very juicy. My question is can tomatoes look good and still be bad?

Duane Marcum, Arizona

Without seeing your jar of tomatoes or knowing your canning process, I'd guess that your tomatoes had what is called "flat sour." Sometimes when a food has flat sour it seems to be sealed, looks okay, but either smells funny or tastes horrible. Some of the reasons for flat sour are: Allowing foods to set in the jars too long before processing (work quickly and process very soon after filling the jars), slow cooling of the jars after processing, like letting them sit in the water bath canner after you process them until the water cools, or canning over-mature foods; you didn't do that with green tomatoes, obviously.

Usually you can smell a food that has gone bad with flat sour. To prevent this from happening again, use good canning procedures, then check the seal when you open a jar, look at the product, smell the food, then cook it and smell it again. You should have no more surprises.

Removing skins from tomatoes necessary?

Love your articles and all the great advice you hand out every month. I have a question regarding canning tomatoes. Why do you have to blanch them to take the skins off before canning them or making any sauces? It would seem to me that you could run them through the blender and put a couple of tablespoons of lemon juice in each quart jar before processing and everything should be okay. Also do you have a recipe for tomato soup that tastes like what you can buy in the store?

Dave Kleis, Washington

Yes, you could do that, Dave, but the sauces or tomato purée won't be as nicely colored (it is kind of pinkish) or smooth if you don't skin and peel them. It would also take a long time to can those tomatoes if you put them in the blender, a few at a time. However if you'd like to ready them for canning this way, there's nothing to stop you. It's safe as well as tasty.

When I make tomato soup, I melt 2 Tbsp. margarine in a large sauce pan. Then I add 2 Tbsp. flour, working the two together into a paste. Add 1 pint of tomato purée. Warm up 2 cups whole milk. Do not boil and do not scorch! Add to hot tomato mixture and stir very thoroughly. Add 1 Tbsp. sugar or more to taste. This is very close to the store "cream of tomato" soups. You may also add 1 cup chicken broth in place of a cup of milk; or vary the spices, adding onion powder or a bit of basil if desired.

Canning tomatoes

I would like to know how long canned tomatoes last.
I opened a jar and it tasted good. But another jar went bad. How do I know how long to keep them?

Carolyn Vermeulen, Arizona

Canned tomatoes should keep for years and years, provided that they were canned correctly. The jar that went bad probably had a bad seal. Just check the seal of a jar before you open it. If it is firmly indented in the center, look at the tomatoes. If they look and smell okay, they are okay to eat, regardless of age. I know I have tomatoes in my pantry that are 15 years old, and I have no hesitations in serving them tomorrow. This is one of the greatest benefits of canning for long-term food storage.

The enemies of long-term tomato storage are dampness and rust. Always remove your rings after your processed jars have cooled. They do not help the seal stay sealed. But they may collect tomato residue from processing or dampness. Either will cut the shelf life of the jars, drastically.

Bubbles in tomatoes

I recently canned my garden tomatoes for the first time and for the most part it went smoothly. My only problem is that after processing (in a hot water bath), there are small air bubbles throughout some of the jars. I used a rubber spatula to get the bubbles out prior to processing, and they looked bubble-free then. My main concern is health; do I need to worry about bacteria?

Kristen Lindberg, New York

No, Kristen, you don't have to worry about small bubbles in your jars, as long as the jar is sealed properly. Press your finger on the center of each lid. (Don't do this until the jar is cooled.) When the jar is sealed, there is no give; it doesn't go down, then pop back up. If it's tight, your tomatoes are perfectly fine. The more you can, the more relaxed you'll be with it.

Acidic tomatoes

Every year my husband and I grow tomatoes in our greenhouse from seed and every fall I can them into toma-

to sauce. I follow canning instructions from the "Ball Blue Book" but the sauce always seems to taste very acidic, almost to the point of being unenjoyable. I use Roma tomatoes specifically grown for saucing, such as Saucy Paste, sold by Irish Eyes Garden Seeds (a great company here in the northwest). What can I do to reduce the acidic taste of my tomato sauce?

Jennifer Smith, Montana

I doubt that your problem has anything to do with your canning or your tomato variety. Here's my best guess. Do you boil your tomato sauce down in a large aluminum or iron stew pot? I did this once and that sauce was terrible. The tomato acid reacts to aluminum and iron, giving that awful taste.

If your tomato sauce is simply too acidic for your taste, you can add about a tablespoon of brown sugar to each pint of sauce expected. You can stir this in well after the sauce is nearly cooked down. It does not affect the processing. Much tomato sauce today has high fructose corn syrup added to it to relieve the taste that is perceived by many as being too acidic. (And, today, most people are conditioned to accept sugar and salt in large amounts in nearly everything.) Good luck in this year's saucing.

Best canning tomato

I always love seeing what you're up to on your homestead in the wilderness!

Just wanted to know what canning tomato you would suggest for a short growing season, hot days, and cool nights.

Robin Balczewski, Washington

We have consistent luck with Oregon Spring, Early Goliath, and Tomcat. But even though we only have about 100 days of frost-free growing, our use of Wallo' Waters lets us harvest plenty of 90 day-plus tomatoes like Gold Medal, Polish Linguisa, and others.

Canned tomatoes

Will canned tomatoes keep two or three years, and how can we tell if they go bad?

Charles Avezzi, Maine

Yes. Canned tomatoes will keep two or three … or 15 years, just fine, providing they are kept in a cool, relatively dark, dry place. This is one of the benefits of home canning. You just keep putting all that great food in your storage pantry for a day you may really need it. Some years the tomato crop is great. Some years something may happen to ruin it, such as hail, drought, or your cow running through the garden. I always can all I am able, for next year, who knows what may happen?

For instance, this year we sold our homestead in the mountains of Montana and moved to our wild homestead in northern Minnesota. Here, beyond the border of the Superior National Forest, there are no buildings, no worked up garden. Only a rocky, gravelly hill overlooking miles of woods and a pretty awesome creek and beaver pond. But that won't grow great tomatoes this summer. So I have lots of them canned up from last year to see us by until we get our new garden worked up to support us.

Canning tomato sauce in half-gallon jars

I have been reading all the issues by Jackie Clay on canning in Backwoods Home Magazine. *I am new at canning this year. I have the books,* Putting Food By, Stocking Up, Ball Blue Book, Keeping The Harvest *and* Canning and Preserving Without Sugar. *None of these books give recipes on canning in half-gallon jars. I would like a recipe for canning tomato sauce in a half-gallon jar and a canning recipe for chili in a half-gallon jar and a bean soup recipe in a half-gallon jar. The information I have read says that half-gallon jars are not good for low-acid food because the food does not cook correctly. I read that Jackie Clay cans using half-gallon jars.*

I enjoy all of BHM *as does my husband. I especially look forward to reading anything that Jackie Clay writes on self-sufficiency. Thank you for your wonderful magazine.*

Darlene and Bob Feener

Yep, all the experts today advise against canning with one to two gallon jars. The reason for this is that some folks got into trouble by packing those huge jars full of cold or lukewarm food, then processing them the exact time ... which "used to be" recommended by the Ball and Kerr canning booklets.

When I began canning a "few" years back, information was included in all the canning "how-to's" for using half-gallon jars. So I just followed the directions, which required a longer period of processing time. This was given as 20% longer processing over the time required for quarts for meats and vegetables, which are of course canned in a pressure canner. Fruits, which are canned in a pressure canner using a half-gallon jar, need an extra five minutes, and when canned in a water bath canner they require an extra ten minutes processing time.

Now, I don't recommend anyone use half-gallon canning jars, but I do use them, and have for years. I do use common sense, and when using them for meat and vegetables, and mixes such as chili and soups, I am absolutely sure that the item is boiling hot when it goes into the (hot) jars and is processed immediately. I'm sure if one were to put cold or merely warm chili into half-gallon jars and exhaust the canner half-heartedly (so that steam was not shouting out the ports, only spitting out from time to time), they could run into trouble with improperly processed food that could spoil or cause health problems.

But as I've often said, I've canned for over 30 years, thousands of jars every year, and never poisoned any diner at my table! One of the bonuses of canning is the convenience of "instant" meals. And half-gallon jars allow quick canning of large meals-in-a-jar. Just check each lid and the appearance of the product before opening to make sure the lid is sealed (indented in the center) and the food looks normal. Then sniff for any off odors. If it's fine, simmer for 15 minutes just to be sure. And enjoy.

But out of legality, remember I didn't advise or recommend that anyone use half-gallon jars for home canning. Everyone is trying their best to keep us safe from ourselves, including home economists and canning companies, and a lot of folks are sue-happy, as well.

Canned tomato sauce without lemon juice

I just canned some tomato sauce and forgot to add the salt and lemon juice. I'm not concerned about the salt, but do I need to worry about the lack of lemon juice? I think that the tomatoes are high acid enough, but thought I would ask your opinion. Do I need to add the lemon juice and reprocess them?

Bob Windsor

To be absolutely safe, you should immediately open those jars as soon as you realize you made a mistake. But, if they were my jars, I would just mark them with an "X" in permanent marker and make sure I didn't use the tomato sauce for a recipe that doesn't require bringing to a boiling temperature for at least 15 minutes and give the sauce an extra good look and sniff test on opening each jar. While it is possible for low-acid tomato sauce to develop harmful bacteria, the chances of it actually happening are quite low. Now this is just how I would handle your situation, of course.

Recanning tomatoes

My wife and I bought an 8-quart pressure cooker/canner from Presto. The regulator weight has one setting: for 15 pounds. Of course the unit comes with an instruction booklet, but it is not terribly detailed. All the recipes in the "Ball Blue Book" and "Putting Food By" use 10 pounds as a reference for most foods. Is there a way to adjust the time to process, or do you know of any way we can adjust the cooker to 10 pounds? Using a different regulator weight?

My next question concerns recanning foods. I know that you can't refreeze food, but are there any health risks of recanning? I have recently used tomatoes that we canned earlier this summer to make a batch of spaghetti sauce and then I canned about 15 quarts of that.

We had some huge tomato plants, over 8 feet high. There was a lot of foliage, but I think the yield was relatively small. We had 5 containers of tomatoes, one pepper and one cucumber. Should I have pruned the plants? How do you do this? I did pinch off the suckers all season. The soil was quite a bit of manure and good dirt. We also took vegetable waste that we puréed up in a blender to feed the tomatoes about once a week. We had a ton of green tomatoes at the end of the season and made 15 pints of chow chow (a relish condiment made with green tomatoes).

But I really would have liked more ripe tomatoes.

Chuck and Denise Cline

You know, I think I would call the Presto Customer Service Department (number on your instruction booklet). The pressure cooker/canner that I think you bought is meant to be used primarily for a pressure cooker, but they advertise it as a canner, also. A larger unit is primarily a canner, meant for that purpose. Perhaps you could use a 10-pound weight, sold with the larger canner. But I wouldn't do it until talking to the Presto folks. Just in case.

No problem in recanning food other than a slight loss of nutrients. And I think that home canning fresh foods quickly and then recanning them would be about equal to the store cans of foods that have been picked over or underripe, hauled and mauled, stored for lengthy times, then canned. I recan foods all the time, as time allows. I, too, can tomato sauce, then later recan it, adding meat, making spaghetti sauce, soups, stews, chili, etc. I even have bought #10 cans very cheaply and recanned smaller jars of the store canned food. For instance, I bought #10 cans of pie cherries at a discount grocery for 99¢ a can, and recanned them into pint jars. They turned out just fine. As for the tomatoes from Jack and the Beanstalk-land, I'd guess that you might have a combination of a fairly late variety of tomato and a heavily fertilized plot. Using a very fertile, manured garden plot, heavy with nitrogen, will make for huge plants, with lots of leaves but little fruit. I'd wager a guess that by the time your plant used up the excess nitrogen and "got down to business," the season was just about over. Ditto for the one cucumber and single pepper. Sounds awfully suspicious, to me.

This year, I'd work the soil up well, and not fertilize it at all until you have tomatoes beginning to set well. Then as they grow, fertilize accordingly. And you might try a less tall, earlier variety, such as Goliath, Oregon Spring, or Early Cascade.

Tomato sauce

What is the best way to remove seeds from tomatoes for sauce? Also, my recipe calls for adding one tablespoon of vinegar or lemon juice per pint, which seems to ruin the rich tomato taste. Is this really necessary if I'm water bath canning sauce made from Romas? I love your articles and column! Looking forward to more "Starting Over."

Cathy Ostrowski, New York

The reason that most modern recipes for canning tomatoes and tomato sauce say to add lemon juice or vinegar is that with the development of hybrid low-acid tomatoes (so that people with touchy stomachs could handle the acid), it also made them too low-acid to can without the added acid (lemon juice or vinegar). Yes, you can water bath old-fashioned Roma tomatoes without the lemon juice or vinegar. Or any other high-acid tomatoes. The reason they say to add the lemon juice or vinegar is that many people don't understand "acid tomatoes or low-acid." To them, a tomato is a tomato, and this makes sure the home canned tomatoes are acidic enough to can safely. I grow only high-acid tomatoes and do not add the vinegar or lemon juice. (Now watch the letters from experts nailing me!)

To get the seeds out of your tomatoes for sauce, the very best method is using a Victorio food mill. This is sort of like a hand meat grinder; handle that you turn, it clamps onto your counter, and has a bin you put tomatoes into. You do not have to peel the tomatoes, so this is a real labor saver when you are canning bushels of tomatoes. You simply cut the stem and core out, cut in two or more pieces (if you don't, they spray juice everywhere!) and then turn the handle. The seeds and skins come out one place and the purée comes out another. You can even recycle the seeds/ skin and get more purée.

This is one gadget I love! But if you can't afford one, you can use an old Foley mill which has a top hand crank (you need to peel the tomatoes). The purée is forced through holes in the bottom. Even rubbing the softened tomatoes through a screen or kitchen sieve will work, although it is a lot more work.

Ask Jackie

Canning tomato sauce

I tried using a vacuum sealer for a batch of sauce I made. What a mistake. It didn't seal tight enough and of course I had to throw it all out. How long do you need to 'bath' the larger 24 oz. jars? I've never tried doing my sauce but I would like to avoid using so much freezer space.

Sharon Baker, Arizona

Canning tomato sauce is so easy. I can't imagine doing anything else with it. And once it's canned, it lasts for years right on your pantry shelf with no more fuss.

To can your sauce, simply pour your seasoned sauce (taste it first!) into warm, clean quart jars, wipe the rim of the jar clean with a warm, damp cloth, then place hot, previously boiled new lids on the jars, tightening down the rings firmly tight. Process them in a boiling water bath canner, with the water at least an inch over the tops of the jars, for 40 minutes, unless you live at an altitude which requires longer processing. Check your canning manual for instructions if you live at an altitude over 1,000 feet above sea level.

When the time is up, remove the jars from the canner and place on a dry folded bath towel to cool. Do not touch the jars until they are cool. Do not re-tighten the rings, poke at the center of the lids, or wipe off any-thing from the jar tops until they are cool to the touch. When they are cool, usually overnight or for several hours, you may remove the rings and wash the jars to remove any sticky or mineral residue from your boil-ing water. This will not cause them to unseal. Remove the rings, because they can sometimes cause the lids to rust.

Canning pizza sauce

I was wondering if you have a recipe for canning pizza sauce?

Linda Moffett

Sure thing, Linda. Often, though, I just mass-can thick tomato sauce, and when I want a pizza for dinner, I add my spices then. This is a labor saver for me during the rush of canning season; I just bake tons and tons of tomato sauce in huge pots, all at once. But here's a pizza sauce you'll enjoy. Please feel free to tailor the spices to fit your preferences. It doesn't affect the canning process at all.

Pizza sauce:

10 lbs. tomatoes

4 cloves garlic, mashed

2 tsp. rubbed oregano

1 tsp. black pepper

2 tsp. basil

3 cups chopped onions

3 Tbsp. olive oil

1 Tbsp. salt

3 Tbsp. brown sugar

½ tsp. chili paste (or ground red pepper)

Peel the tomatoes and remove stems. Chop. I run mine through a Victorio food mill, which does everything in one process, including mashing the chopped onions. This is a really handy homestead tool. If you don't have one available, simmer the chopped onions and tomatoes for about 20 minutes along with the other ingredients in a large pot. Then run the sauce through a sieve or food mill. Return to the pot and simmer, stirring frequently to avoid scorching the bottom and cook down till about half the volume.

If you are not sure your tomatoes are acidic, add 1 tsp. of lemon juice to each pint jar of sauce.

Pour hot into hot pint jars, leaving ¼ inch of headroom. Wipe the rims of the jars clean with a damp cloth. Place hot, previously boiled lids on the jars and screw down the rings firmly tight. Process pints 35 minutes in boiling water bath. This makes about three pints of pizza sauce. You can certainly double or triple these amounts for serious canning. Just make sure you stir the final purée, as it does tend to scorch as it gets thick.

Canning catsup

I am looking for a tomato catsup recipe that I may use fresh or can. I find only fancy recipes that my husband wouldn't care for, or catsup made from cukes. I know that you have a good answer to my question. I want you to know that I have been using a canning guide that was published in the mid '80s and after seeing you mention "a new or recent canning guide, like Ball's Blue Book" I went to their web site and found out that canning guidelines changed in 1989, and if your book is older than that you may be using an unsafe technique or timing, so I sent for a copy. Had you not mentioned it so frequently, I would not have had any reason to check their site. You may have helped avert a canning mishap. Thank you.

Janean

Here's a plain old-fashioned catsup recipe that should work for you. It will be very good, but remember that commercial catsup is sweetened with corn syrup, not sugar, so the consistency is smoother and shinier than sugar-sweetened catsup. But homemade catsup is really great and easy to do, too.

Homemade catsup:

> 1 gallon of tomatoes
> 1 medium onion
> 1 Tbsp. pickling spices
> 2 tsp. salt
> 1 cup sugar
> 1 cup vinegar

Peel and chop the tomatoes and onion. You may put the tomatoes through a Victorio food mill. Put into a large enameled or stainless steel pot. Add the pickling spices, tied in a bag. Simmer until soft. Put through strainer to remove seeds and tough pulp. Remove the pickling spices. Place in jelly bag and hang over a bowl until the pulp is the right consistency. Add the salt, sugar, and vinegar. Boil 20 minutes, stirring frequently to avoid scorching. When the right thickness, pour into hot clean pint jars, wipe the rims clean, and place hot, previously boiled lid on and screw down the ring firmly tight. Process in a boiling water bath canner for 15 minutes.

Watery tomato sauce

I have written before and I have to say that I love all the answers. We are currently getting all the veggies in the ground and so far we are seeing blooms on the Early Girl tomatoes! Yay! Only one question with that. Last year I canned all this wonderful tomato sauce that I thought would be great. Just had to pour it out and heat it up for noodles and meatballs. But it was not to be. The sauce was basically watery and tasteless. What can I do to make it better this year? Can I make the recipe but not cook it down and just pack it in hot jars? Without water? And process it in a water canner?

Jonica Kelly, Maryland

I'm not sure what you did with your sauce. To make great tomato sauce, first either peel your tomatoes or run them through a tomato strainer like a Victorio food mill. Purée the tomatoes, one way or another, *not* adding water. Then add any spices you wish, just like you were making your sauce from fresh. If you don't know if your tomatoes are an acidic variety, add 1 Tbsp. lemon juice to each pint jar and 2 Tbsp. to each quart jar before you fill them. Simmer the tomato sauce down until it is fairly thick; the thickness depends on your likes but remember the lemon juice will slightly water it down. Process. This sauce will *not* be watery and tasteless.

Acidic tomato sauce

*In issue 89, on page 71, a letter on acidic tomatoes —
the solution is simple. Instead of sugar, and depending on
the quantity of the tomato sauce, use a half teaspoon to a
teaspoon of baking soda (sodium bicarbonate) and mix. It
is a simple chemical reaction of neutralizing the acidity of
the tomato sauce. But if you use too much baking soda you
will ruin the taste of the sauce, so try a little at a time until
it tastes right.*

Robert D'Andrea, New Jersey

Yes, Robert, you're right. You can use the baking soda
instead of sugar. I've found that most folks prefer the additional sugar to the sauce with the baking soda, but it's
probably not good for us.

Adding vinegar to tomato sauce

*Can you help me with a couple of canning questions? Last
season my wife and I had 14 tomato plants that produced
mountains of awesome tomatoes. We started making salsa,
sauce, freezing, and drying. All the canning instructions
for tomato products have you add vinegar, which promptly
destroys the flavor. None of the commercial products have
vinegar. Is there a way I can check the acid level so I can
only add just enough vinegar? Or can I just pressure can
them? I haven't been able to find a pressure canning recipe
for tomatoes. Also, do you have a recipe for canning dried
tomatoes in olive oil?*

Jonathan Burson

The reason most modern canning instructions have you
add vinegar is that some newer varieties of tomatoes are

151

bred to be low-acid, making them, supposedly, easier to digest for people who normally can't eat tomatoes because of stomach upsets from the acid. But those low-acid tomatoes make canning them a bit risky, as one reason you can water bath process tomatoes safely is that they are a high-acid food.

I don't use vinegar for sauces and salsa, but I do raise all my own plants from seeds and I only plant old-fashioned high-acid tomato varieties, never the low-acid varieties. When choosing your varieties for the garden, read a few garden catalogs and jot down a list of low-acid varieties and shy away from them for canning.

One gets into a bind when buying bulk canning tomatoes, instead of raising them, as you just can't look at a tomato and know which it is. Thus the "add vinegar" concept was born just in case. Commercial processors often use citric acid instead of vinegar. You can use ¼ tsp. per pint. I have used lemon juice, instead of vinegar, on occasion. You will use two Tbsp. bottled lemon juice per pint. But, like I said, I much prefer using plain old high-acid natural tomatoes and not buying lemon juice, citric acid, or vinegar.

You do have to be careful when canning salsa, to either use a proven recipe or to pressure can, using the time for the "longest" ingredient, usually peppers, as some folks add too many onions and peppers for the acid to keep the harmful bacteria in check if using a water bath canner.

No, I don't have a recipe for canning dried tomatoes in olive oil. Oil is an enemy of home canning as it often boils between the jar lid and rim, making a good seal difficult. Until we can find a recipe, you can do as we do and make up a few jars at a time, replacing as you use them. They stay good in a cool place on the counter quite a while. Or you can place them in the fridge if you prefer.

Canning salsa

I am wanting to can salsa using tomatoes, pepper, onions, and garlic. I'm not sure if I can give them the hot water bath, or if I have to pressure cook them.

Becke Treas, Texas

You have to be a little careful with salsas, making sure that you have an acidic enough product. What you can do is to look at the basic salsa recipes in the *Ball Blue Book* canning manual for amounts of tomatoes, peppers, onions, etc., along with any vinegar or lemon juice added for extra acidity. Then just adjust the spices to suit your own tastes. You need to keep the acidity up so you can process your salsas in a water bath canner. This keeps the vegetables tasting "fresh" instead of "cooked," as they would if you pressure canned them. You can pick up a *Ball Blue Book* canning handbook at any store that carries canning supplies, including Wal-Mart, for a low cost. Good salsa making! I make several different ones, including a corn and black bean salsa.

Salsa recipe

I'm hoping you can help me, since Backwoods Home Magazine *seems to be one of the few places where I've found anything about canning. I'm growing tomatoes, cilantro and jalapeños in my backyard. I've planted this stuff for salsa in my garden, and have no recipe to follow!*

Eric Kiefer, Pennsylvania

Ask Jackie

Salsa is like a marriage — no two are alike. I'll enclose a basic recipe, but you'll have to taste it while it's fresh and adjust the cilantro and spices to your liking. The only thing that is "a must" is the processing time. I used to process my salsas in a hot water bath canner, but now use a pressure canner, as it is possible to use too many low-acid veggies, such as onions and peppers, for the hot water bath canner. A pressure canner provides needed safety, just in case.

Salsa:

> 40 medium tomatoes
> 5 cups finely chopped onions
> 4 cups finely chopped celery
> 2 cups finely chopped jalepeños (may use
>   other peppers, to taste)
> ½ cup lemon or lime juice
> ½ cup finely chopped cilantro
> 5 Tbsp. salt

To peel tomatoes, dip in boiling water a few at a time for 30 seconds, plunge into cold water, then slip the skins off. Chop the veggies fine, add other ingredients in large pot. Bring to boil. You may add sugar to taste, if desired. Pour into hot jars, seal. Process pints 25 minutes at 10 pounds pressure. (Adjust the pressure, if needed, due to altitude.)

Recanning salsa

I canned several pints of salsa last year. It was so pretty, but not nearly hot enough. I am wondering if I can empty the jars into a large pot, add more jalapeños, and re-can in a boiling water bath? Also, I got really tired at the end of the season last year and froze whole jalapeños instead of canning them. Would it be okay to use those?

Lana Getto, Indiana

I wouldn't recan the salsa; it would get pretty soft, and salsa is best chunky. What I'd do is when I open a jar, I'd add enough chili paste to each jar to make it hot enough to suit you. Chili paste can be found in Oriental markets or in the Mexican or Oriental sections of most large grocery stores. The brand I like is Sambal Oelek without garlic. It is very mellow and wonderful tasting. A jar lasts for months in the fridge. I use it a lot in a wide variety of recipes. Yes, you can use the frozen jalapeños, but be aware that they won't be firm when added to salsa, like fresh ones would be. Personally, I'd use the frozen jalapeños for other recipes and use fresh ones for your salsa.

Canning V8 style juice

After Hurricane Katrina and losing the contents of our freezer and refrigerator, I am purchasing a pressure canner for future preserving. I've only done water bath preserving in the past, and I know that tomatoes have a high enough acidity to be able to water bath can tomato juice, but what about homemade V8 style with other vegetable juices in them?

Therese Hirko, Mississippi

Glad you weathered the storm. And I'm happy to hear you're getting a pressure canner to put up food for future emergencies and happier times, too.

Luckily, you can safely process V8 style juice in a water bath canner. Here's a recipe that is safe, and good too.

V8 style juice:

> 25 lbs. tomatoes
> ¾ cup diced carrots
> ¾ cup chopped celery
> ¾ cup chopped bell peppers
> ½ cup chopped onion
> ¼ cup chopped parsley
> 1 Tbsp. salt (optional)

Remove core of tomatoes and cut into large chunks. Combine with other ingredients in large pot and simmer, stirring often. Simmer 20 minutes. Run through a food mill or sieve to remove skins and seeds of tomatoes and mash other vegetables. Add salt. Reheat juice to 190°F. Pour into hot pint or quart jars. To each quart, add 2 Tbsp. lemon juice; to each pint, 1 Tbsp. Leave ¼ inch of headspace. Process pints for 35 minutes and quarts for 40 minutes in a hot water bath.

I, too, began canning nearly all my food when a week-long storm took out the power and I lost a lot of the food in my freezer; not a nice thing to have happen to you. You'll like many things home canned better than frozen. And once you put food in those jars, it's good. No power outages, freezer burn, or other loss will steal your hard earned food.

Recipe for V8 juice

I really appreciate all of the help that so many others and I get from your column each time we open an issue of Backwoods Home Magazine. *I have learned so much from you and I look forward to learning even more. Thank you once again for telling me how to make vinegar in the Sept/Oct. issue.*

Okay, now to my next question. Do you have a recipe to make V8 juice? I would like to know what all the vegetables they use are, and how I would go about canning it.

Zeldon Linn, Oregon

Be glad to help you Zeldon. Here's a recipe that I like.

Homesteader's V8:

22 lbs. tomatoes
2 quarts celery, chopped
2 beets, chopped
¾ cup carrots, chopped
¾ cup onions, chopped
¾ cup green pepper, chopped
¼ cup chopped parsley
bottled lemon juice
salt (optional)

Remove core and blossom ends of tomatoes. Cut into quarters or smaller. Chop all vegetables. Add tomatoes and vegetables in a large kettle. Slowly bring to a simmer and simmer 20 minutes, stirring to prevent sticking. Mash the vegetables as they begin to soften. Run the purée through a food mill to remove skins and seeds. Stir in salt to taste if desired. Heat juice 5 minutes to simmering; do not boil. Ladle hot juice into hot jars, leaving ½ inch of headspace. Add 1 Tbsp. bottled lemon juice to pint jars, and 2 Tbsp. to quart jars. Process pints for 35 minutes in a boiling water bath and quarts for 40 minutes.

Peppers

Canning peppers

My wife and I have a 50x100-foot garden with a lot of habañeros, serrano and cayenne peppers. How do you can them?

Jay Helton

I prefer to dry cayenne peppers, then powder them to use in recipes as you use very little of them at one time. You can do this with habañeros as well, but I'd seed them first as they are fire to eat with seeds.

I like to pickle jalapeños and serranos, and you might like to do that with habañeros, too. That way, you can use the peppers in recipes, salads, as a snack, and use the vinegar, which becomes spicy and flavorful, too. And they sure are pretty in the jars. Just be sure to use plastic or rubber gloves

159

when working with them as your fingers, especially under the nails, quickly begin to burn, and you can't put the fire out.

Pickling hot peppers is easy. Cut slits in each pepper with a small, sharp knife. Over four quarts of peppers, pour four quarts of water, into which 1½ cups of canning salt has been dissolved. Let this stand, covered, overnight in a cool place. In the morning, drain and rinse. Combine in large saucepan: 10 cups vinegar, ¼ cup sugar (optional), 2 cups water and bring to a boil. Pack the peppers into hot, sterile jars, leaving ¼ inch of headspace. Pour the boiling liquid over peppers, just covering them, and leaving ¼ inch of headspace. Wipe the rims and seal. Process pints for 10 minutes in a boiling water bath, quarts for 15 minutes. (Adjust the time if you're over 1,000 feet above sea level.)

Giving mild/sweet peppers a "bite"

I purchased mild/sweet peppers in error. I have just cut and cleaned a bushel and I want to can them and give them a bite. What can I do with them to make them have a bite? I normally can Hungarian mild/leaning toward hot and try to mellow them. I am now faced with trying to make them hotter. I could try adding some pepper chips but I do not want to waste the whole lot. Please advise.

Mary Hulewicz

If you want a real zing in those oh-so-mild peppers, try canning them with two or three habañeros in each pint. These little dandies are so hot that they'll fire up everything they come in contact with. If you don't want that much heat, drop one or two dried hot peppers in each jar, as you would hot dill pickles. We don't want you to catch fire.

Canning chile peppers

I would like to can chile peppers. I had an overabundance of them this year. My family likes to make things with them in. But I have only found pickle peppers. There has to be a recipe for them.

Kammi VanderZiel

Sure you can home can chile peppers. I can them every time I have enough, as I use the canned roasted peppers in a lot of recipes. My favorite is scrambled eggs with chiles in them, topped with melted cheddar and crunchy toast.

To can them, first roast them for best taste. This is easily done by laying the peppers on your grill over hot coals, not flames, until the skins blister and begin to blacken. Roll them over and do the other side. You can also roast them in your oven on a cookie sheet at 400°F, but the grill tastes best (especially if you use mesquite or fruit tree wood). After they are roasted, quickly place them in a paper sack and roll the top shut. Leave them in it until they are cool. This helps the skins peel off easily. Remove the skins and seeds, if desired. Removing the seeds reduces somewhat the fire of the chile. Wear rubber gloves or the area under your fingernails will burn like heck for days. I don't, and mine do.

Pack the chiles in half-pint jars, then fill the jar to within half an inch of the top with boiling water. Half a teaspoon of salt may be added, if desired. Process the jars in a pressure canner for 35 minutes at 10 pounds pressure, unless you live at an altitude above 1,000 feet, in which case, consult your canning manual for directions on adjusting your pressure to correspond with your altitude.

Making hot sauce

I got a recipe for making hot sauce off the internet. It told me to put the peppers in a solution of salt water for a month and then add vinegar.

Then I am supposed to strain it and that's it. My problem is that there is a moldy covering over the sauce and I am afraid of it. The sauce has been covered the entire time as the recipe called for that. Is it supposed to have a covering of mold over it?

Debbie Hayes, Alabama

This recipe is probably a Tabasco take-off of the original Tabasco process that is still used today. But, as you've found, it can be a little tricky if the peppers aren't kept pressed down in the salt brine. You need to keep them totally under it, pressed down with a plastic bag filled with water or a sterile plate, weighted down. Here is an easier recipe that will give you good, dependable results:

> 36 Tabasco peppers — or other long hot red
>   peppers
> 1 clove garlic
> 1 Tbsp. sugar
> ½ tsp. salt
> 1 cup hot vinegar
> 1 cup water

❦   ❦   ❦   ❦   ❦   ❦   ❦

Add water to the peppers and garlic. Cook in a medium pan until tender, then press through fine sieve. Add all other ingredients and simmer until blended. Pour into hot jars, leaving ¼ inch of headspace. Process in a boiling water bath canner for 15 minutes. If you live at an altitude above 1,000 feet, consult your canning book for directions on increasing your processing time to suit your altitude, if necessary.

❦   ❦   ❦   ❦   ❦   ❦   ❦

Canning chiles and sauce

My questions are about pressure canning red and green chiles. How long do you do the green chile? The same as bell peppers? When I tried to make red sauce and canned it, it seemed to darken a whole lot. How can I keep the brighter red color? Do you have specific recipes for these I could try? How about for home canned enchilada sauces (both red and green)? We eat a lot of chile products and I am trying to keep it without freezing due to high electric costs. Any other chile preserving tips would be welcome (besides freezing).

Cindy Barnett, Arizona

You process green chiles for 30 minutes for pints and half-pints. Bell peppers are processed longer because they are thicker-meated than chiles. To keep a brighter red color, try adding a Tbsp. lemon juice to each pint or a tsp. to each half-pint. This often helps your red sauce stay red.

Any recipe for enchilada sauce will can up perfectly. My friend, Jeri, recently made up her own recipe for an enchilada sauce she'd previously bought at the store by just reading the label and experimenting with amounts. She got it right the first time and now cans up big batches at a time. I'm sorry I'm not a "recipe" person. To make something, I just add what I know it has in it and keep tasting until it's like I want it to taste. Tomato sauce, chile, onion, cilantro, lemon, or lime? Maybe a little bit of oregano?

The main thing is to always can for the ingredient needing the most processing time. For instance, when you add more chiles than just to flavor your tomato sauce, you *must* pressure can it for safety.

Don't forget about drying chiles. They keep very well for years and are oh so handy in the kitchen. Nearly every southwestern kitchen should have a *rista* hanging in the kitchen handy for use.

Canning jalapeños

How do you can jalapeños?

Donna Guthrie, Alabama

You can home can jalapeños just like you would any other pepper, by pressure canning them. But most folks prefer them pickled to retain the crunch. I do for sure.

To can them, you first remove the stem, core, and seeds, wearing rubber gloves to keep from getting your fingers burned. Remove the skins by dropping them in boiling water for a few minutes, then dipping them out and plunging them into cold. Or you can roast them on the grill until the skins are blackened in spots, then place in a bag to steam for a few minutes. Again, plunge them into cold water to loosen the skins. Peel. Then pack into hot jars. Add 1 tsp. salt to each pint or

½ tsp. to each half-pint. Also add 1 Tbsp. vinegar to each pint. Ladle boiling water over peppers, leaving 1 inch of headspace. Remove air bubbles. Process half-pints and pints for 35 minutes at 10 pounds pressure (unless you live at an altitude over 1,000 feet and must adjust your pressure to suit your altitude; consult your canning book for directions.)

As I've said, most folks pickle them instead, as it retains the crunch; pressure canned jalapeños get kind of soft. To pickle them, you will need a gallon of peppers, 1½ cups pickling salt, 1 gallon water, 2 Tbsp. sugar, 1 cup water, and 5 cups vinegar.

Wash and drain peppers. Cut 2 small slits in each pepper. Dissolve salt in 1 gallon cold water. Pour over peppers. Let stand overnight in cool place. Rinse and drain. Add sugar and 1 cup vinegar. Simmer 15 minutes. Pack peppers into hot, sterilized jars. Pour boiling pickling liquid over peppers, leaving ½ inch of headspace. Remove air bubbles. Process in a boiling water bath canner for 15 minutes. If you live at an altitude over 1,000 feet, consult your canning book for directions on increasing your processing time to suit your altitude, if necessary.

Canning stuffed peppers

Do you have a recipe for pressure canning stuffed peppers? I have looked everywhere.

Gloria J. Hemontolor, Tennessee

165

Ask Jackie

I basically make up my own stuffed pepper recipe: hamburger, rice, tomato sauce, and spices. Then I bake them in a tomato sauce until they are partially done and very hot. These are carefully packed into hot wide-mouth pint jars, two to a jar. I add boiling tomato sauce to within an inch of the top. These are processed for 75 minutes at 10 pounds pressure. If you live at an altitude over 1,000 feet, check your canning manual for directions on adjusting your pressure to suit your altitude.

Nuts and legumes

Basics of canning nuts

I would like to know how to pressure can walnuts or any other nut.

Elaine Rolfs, Iowa

Nuts are very easy to can and keep a lot longer than those kept in bags or cans without going rancid.

To can nuts, first shell them, then lay them out in a single layer on cookie sheets and put them in your oven at about 250°F to toast. Stir them once in a while to keep them from scorching, and toast them for about 25 minutes or until they are very dry, but not browning.

167

Pack them into hot, *dry* jars, leaving ½ inch of head-space. Wipe the rim of the jars clean and place a hot, previously simmered *dry* lid on and screw the ring down firmly tight. Process at five pounds pressure for 10 minutes in your pressure canner.

You'll really love having these canned nuts available (and not rancid) in your pantry.

Canning chestnuts

How do I put up/prepare chestnuts? I'm guessing they can be canned, but will need instructions. I also don't remember how long to oven roast them.

Mary Wolfe, Pennsylvania

Yes, you can home can chestnuts and other nutmeats.

Peel your chestnuts and lay them in a single layer on a cookie sheet in your oven. You can boil or steam the chestnuts first to make peeling easier, then roast them. Slowly roast them at 250°F, turning them to prevent scorching — they'll dry out nicely. You want all the nutmeats hot for packing. Pack hot into hot jars, leaving ½ inch of headroom at the top of the jar. Use either pint or half-pint jars only. Process the jars at 5 pounds pressure for 10 minutes (unless you live at an altitude above 1,000 feet, then adjust for your altitude; check your canning manual). You'll note that this pressure is different from the usual 10 pounds that most other foods are processed at.

Canning gravy and nuts

I am wondering if it is possible to can homemade gravies successfully. If made from scratch, what would be the times to process if made from butter, a by product of animals, or from animal fats itself?

Can I can salted nuts successfully? I have done the unsalted and they are very good — in fact, people asked me where did I get them as they were so fresh!

Linda Oehlke, Wisconsin

A light gravy can be canned as if you were processing meat broth, but any gravy that is quite thick should not be canned. Wait to thicken it further upon use.

You can salt your nuts before canning. Salt is only for flavor, and has nothing to do with the canning. You can even add other flavors to your nuts, such as hot peppers, herbs, or spices.

Canning pecans

I'm looking for a way to can pecans in a warm oven. What temperature and what time? Supposed to lightly screw the lid on and leave overnight in warm oven. Do you know?

Katie Daffin, Louisiana

Oven canning isn't recommended for safe sealing of canned nutmeats. Instead, dry your pecans on a cookie sheet in an oven set at 250°F. Stir them a few times and continue heating for about half an hour. Pack them into hot pint or half-pint jars with no liquid. Pressure can them at 5 pounds pressure for 10 minutes. You can also water bath process nutmeats for 30 minutes, but they will float, as they have a lot of air space in them.

Shelling and canning pecans

I have pecans — all that we want — for free. I was wondering how I can store them so that they will not go bad without freezing them. Also, can you turn these into pecan peanut butter? And if you can turn these into pecan peanut butter, can you can it? If you can put them in canning jars how would I go about it?

Glenda Gay, Alabama

Boy are you lucky! Pecans are so good! One year, while we lived in New Mexico, our neighbor lady traveled to her son's place down in the southern part of the state and came home with a burlap sack full of pecans. We spent the winter, on and off, yacking in her kitchen, cracking pecans, and picking out nutmeats. Then I brought my share home and canned them. They are really good this way, and now, six years later, they are still good, not rancid. And they are super easy to can, too.

The easiest method I've found for shelling pecans is the nifty little lever action nutcracker that is sold in many garden catalogs. My neighbor had one of these, and they really did a nice job, leaving most of the nutmeats in halves.

Once shelled, spread the nutmeats out on a cookie sheet and put them in the oven at 250°F. You want to toast them, but not brown them. You will stir them once or twice until they are just right. (Taste 'em!)

To can them, you fill the jars to within half an inch of the top, then place a hot, previously boiled, dry lid on the jars, screwing down the ring firmly tight. (Do not add water!) Process them either for 10 minutes at 5 pounds pressure in a pressure canner, or 30 minutes in a water bath canner. This method works for all nutmeats that I can think of.

The pecans will keep quite a while in their shell without going rancid, so there isn't a huge rush in getting them put up.

Canning pecan and walnut meats

I have done a lot of canning, but I am interested in learning how to can pecan and walnut meats. Help! Please.
Connie

Canning nutmeats is very easy and makes them last indefinitely, as opposed to leaving them in the bag or in the shell where they get rancid pretty quickly.

There are several methods, which all seem to work.

Spread the nutmeats in a shallow layer on cookie tins and bake at no more than 250°F, stirring once in a while until dry but not browned. Keep hot until packed. Pack into half-pint or pint jar and pressure can dry for 10 minutes at 5 pounds pressure. Remember to adjust the pounds of pressure for higher altitude, if necessary.

Or you can use a hot water bath for 30 minutes. Can the nutmeats dry; add no liquid.

You'll find that all varieties of nutmeats can up quickly and easily, keeping indefinitely with a wonderful fresh-roasted taste.

Canning nuts

I read an article several years ago where you talked about canning nuts. Can I have these directions again, please? Also, do you answer via email or only in the publication?

Caroline Waldner

Sure, glad to. Nuts are so easy to can; it only takes a few minutes, and little work. Here's how:

Sterilize pint jars by boiling them, then keep dry and hot. Boil your lids and keep them in warm water. Spread your nutmeats out in a single layer on cookie sheets in the oven and toast at 250°F for about 30 minutes, stirring every 10 minutes for even toasting; do not brown. Fill dry, hot, sterilized jars with nutmeats to within ½ inch of the jar top.

Now, the old method, which I've successfully used, is to place the hot lid on the jar, tighten down the ring firmly tight, and place jars into a pan of boiling water, coming to just below the rings. Process for 30 minutes.

I've switched to using a conventional water bath canner, covering the jars, as with other foods. The processing time is the same. No, the nuts do not get wet, provided you screw down those rings firmly tight (without force, though).

Or you can pressure can nutmeats at 5 pounds pressure (adjusting pressure upward for altitude, if necessary; see canning manual for altitude pressure adjustments) for 10 minutes.

See, wasn't that easy?

I only answer questions in *BHM*. I'm old-fashioned and have no computer, only an aging word processor. And I'm

172

also too hugely busy with daily homestead chores and activities to answer via e-mail.

Canning homemade peanut butter

Do you know how to can homemade peanut butter?

Dezarae Graham, Idaho

You can home can homemade peanut butter in widemouth pint jars. Pack it well, with no air bubbles, to within an inch of the top of the jar. Wipe the jar rim clean and place a hot, previously simmered lid on the jar and screw down the ring firmly tight. Process the jars one hour in a hot water bath canner.

Preserving chestnuts

My chestnut trees are loaded with chestnuts this year and I would like to know how I could preserve some of them for winter use. Can you can chestnuts? I thought I read something somewhere about canning chestnuts but I can't remember where or how.

Marion Calhoun, Pennsylvania

Yes, you can can chestnuts and other nutmeats. And it's quick and easy, too.

Just peel your chestnuts and lay them in a single layer on a cookie sheet in your oven. Slowly roast them at 250°F, turning them to prevent scorching. Use two or more pans to make a good big batch for canning at one time. You want all the nutmeats hot for packing. Pack hot into hot jars, leaving ½ inch of headroom at the top of the jar. Use either pint or half-pint jars only. Process the jars at 5 pounds pressure for 10 minutes (unless you live at an altitude above 1,000 feet and must adjust your pressure to suit your altitude, if necessary; check your canning manual). You'll note that this pressure is different from the usual 10 pounds that most other foods are processed at.

You can also process nutmeats in a water bath canner, but do not fill the canner with water higher than the shoulders of the jars. This is one of the only foods that this applies to; most foods have the water level at least 2 inches above the jar tops. But you want absolutely no moisture to enter the jars or the nutmeats might mold.

Can rancid nuts be used?

We have several packages each of shelled walnuts, almonds, peanuts, and pecans stored in large plastic containers in our pantry that have turned rancid. Also, some in jars on the shelves are rancid. The nuts we use regularly are kept in the freezer, and seem to keep a long time without becoming rancid. Is there a way to store them so they won't become rancid? What can be done with the rancid nuts to make them edible again? Have you ever vacuumpacked them?

Jerry Sisler, Montana

Sorry, but there's nothing I know of that will make rancid nuts taste good. I can my nutmeats and they've kept for years in the jars without becoming rancid. They're easy to can, too.

Just put them on a cookie sheet and gently heat them in the oven at 250°F, stirring them to keep them from scorching. When they are hot, place them in hot pint or half-pint canning jars and place a hot, previously simmered lid on the jar and screw the ring down firmly tight. You can water bath process the jars by having the water in the canner ½ inch below the top of the jars and processing them for 30 minutes from the time the water comes back to a rolling boil. Or you can process them in a pressure canner at 6 pounds (dial gauge) or 5 pounds with a weighted gauge, for 10 minutes.

Old dried beans

Jackie, I just found your site and I love it. My question is, I have a lot of dried beans (pintos) in my food storage and they are old, and will not soften up to eat. What can I do with the beans or is there any way they can be used as food?

Gail Robertson

I've had pretty good luck with those old beans by soaking them in boiling water overnight (pour boiling water on the dry beans, then let sit overnight in a cool place), then rinsing, using fresh water, boiling them for an hour, and packing them into canning jars to within an inch of the top. Then I pour the water on to within an inch of the top, adding ½ tsp. salt to pints, 1 tsp. to quarts, then pressure canning them at 10 pounds pressure for 75 minutes for pints or 90 minutes for quarts. (If you live at an altitude above 1,000 feet, consult your canning manual for directions on adjusting your pressure to suit your altitude, if necessary.)

The pre-soaking, boiling, and pressure canning seems to help a great deal. If they still seem tough, pulse through a blender before you use them to make kind of a bean mash; it's good in most recipes calling for pintos, including re-fried beans.

Another way to use them is to make bean flour out of them. Run them through your flour mill or meat grinder to chop them fine, then whiz them in your blender to make bean flour. You can use this in a variety of recipes. It thickens gravies and makes dandy refried beans when you add boiling water and simmer with spices in a pot on the back of the wood stove or in the oven. I'm sure a slow cooker would work too.

Canning dry beans

Although I keep dry beans in my pantry, I would like to know how to can beans for those times when I am in a rush and don't have the time to spend hours cooking the dry beans so they are ready to add to chili or soup. I figure that since I can buy beans in a "tin" can at the store it should be possible using my pressure canner. Can you point me in the right direction? Also, do I need to worry about the beans becoming mushy by canning them in the pressure canner?

Lyn Ankelman, Alabama

You are absolutely right about the convenience of having canned beans in the pantry! And there are several ways to go here. Nearly all bean recipes may be home canned. For instance, I have in my own pantry: canned baked beans, refried beans, bean soup, and chili (three recipes), along with "plain" canned, previously dry beans of four varieties to be quickly used should the need or whim strike me.

And beans are really easy to put up too. Besides, it leaves them tender but not mushy. Like you said, too, it frees you from the soaking and long cooking when you are in a hurry or company drops by. Here's how to do simple canned dry beans:

Cover dry beans (or peas) with cold water and let stand overnight in a cool place. Drain. Cover beans or peas with cold water two inches over the beans in a large saucepan. Bring to a boil and boil half an hour. Stir as needed. Dip out beans with a slotted spoon and pack into hot canning jar to within an inch of the top. Add 1 tsp. salt to quart jars, ½ tsp. to pints, if desired. Ladle hot cooking liquid into jar to within an inch of the top. Remove any air bubbles with a small spatula or wooden stick. Wipe rim of jar clean. Place a hot, previously simmered lid on jar and screw down ring firmly tight. Process pints 75 minutes, quarts 90 minutes in a pressure canner at 10 pounds pressure. If you live at an altitude above 1,000 feet, adjust the pressure to your altitude as recommended in your canning manual.

That's it. See how easy it was!

Most of your homemade bean recipes can likewise be home canned. Just keep the time the same, as beans (like meat) require a longer processing time to render safe to eat.

Recipe for canning dry beans

I've misplaced the issue of BHM *with your advice on canning dry beans. I followed your instructions last year and we've had wonderful meals all winter thanks to you. Could you please remind me of the recipe? Also, do you can black-eyed peas with the same instructions?*

Carmen Black

Glad you enjoyed canned dried beans. They sure are a labor saver, aren't they? And no worries about getting older beans tender! Here's the recipe. And yes, you can do any type of dried beans or peas this way.

Any type of dry bean or pea: Wash beans, soak in cold water overnight. Boil beans 15 minutes. Pack gently in jars to within 2 inches of top. Add 1 tsp. salt to each quart jar. Fill jar to within 1 inch of top with precooking liquid. Wipe jar rim clean, place hot, previously boiled lid on jar and screw down ring firmly tight. Process pints and quarts for one hour at 10 pounds pressure. Adjust pressure, if necessary, according to altitude. See canning manual. (You can also precook the beans in a seasoned tomato juice, which makes the beans similar to store-bought "pork & beans.")

Canning dried beans

In your latest newsletter, you were asked about dried beans — my problem with using more beans has always been that I either forget to soak them the night before, or just don't get around to cooking them most of the time till it is too late.

While browsing, I discovered a blog by someone who had a friend in Texas who showed her how she did beans ...

She washed and picked clean the dried beans and put ⅔ of a cup in each pint (1⅓ for quarts — it figures out to about ¼ pound per pint and ½ pound per quart), added salt and spices to taste — filled with boiling water to leave 1 inch of headspace, wiped rim, put on lids and bands and processed — (I did them at 10 pounds pressure for 75 min. for pints and 90 min. for quarts) I added a bit of ham in some and bacon in others.

Well, it is so easy, after 4 cases of canned beans, my wife asked me if I didn't think that was enough for now ... I was actually hoping there would be a seal failure so I had an excuse to try them, but having none, I was glad I had used the new reusable Tattlers.

So far, I have done pinto beans, black beans, red beans, navy beans and butter beans — using up some of the bags I had stored for several years. They turned out great! Now it is so easy to use them that we are using them several times each week. They process to where they are very tender, just right to mash the pintos for refried beans, just add more water to the navy or butter beans for soup, or straight for black beans or red beans and rice.

Next project — add baked bean ingredients (either molasses or use up tomato juice left over from last year) before processing my dry beans ... maybe a few drops of liquid smoke — then I can just pop them in the crock and into the oven ... Any ingredient suggestions?

Cal Hollis, Delaware

I'm going to try the method you discovered for canning dry beans. What I do is only a little more work; I boil them for a few minutes then let them sit in the water for a couple of hours. Then I pack them and process as usual. They come out nice and tender, and it is a lot easier than waiting overnight.

I can my versions of "baked beans" all the time. I add chopped onions, bits of bacon or ham, tomato juice, and brown sugar. The recipe can be found in my new canning book, *Growing and Canning Your Own Food*, but you can develop your own, too.

Old pinto beans

We have a lot of nitro-packed, 10-year-old pinto beans that we have not been able to cook by conventional methods. How can we soften the beans to cook?
Carthal and Janice Hawks, South Carolina

I have a lot of pintos that I bought when living in New Mexico, 16 years ago, which are stored in gallon jars and popcorn tins. As my beans are old, I also had trouble getting them cooked so they were soft enough to use. So, instead of beating them up by continual boiling, I simply canned them up. (This recipe, along with tons more, of course, is in my new canning book!)

To can them, just rinse the dry beans and sort them, if needed. Cover well with boiling water and bring to a boil for 2 minutes. Remove from heat and let soak, covered for 2 hours. Heat to boiling and drain, saving liquid. Pack jars ¾ full with hot beans. Add small pieces of fried lean bacon or ham, if desired. (For pintos, I simmered the liquid briefly with chopped onion and powdered chiles to give the beans more flavor.)

Fill jars with hot cooking liquid, leaving 1 inch of headspace. Process pints for 65 minutes and quarts for 75 minutes at 10 pounds pressure in a pressure canner. If you live at an altitude above 1,000 feet, consult your canning book for directions on increasing your pressure to suit your altitude, if necessary.

This results in soft beans that can either be served as is or mashed and made into the best frijoles possible!

Canning black beans

I'm interested in canning black beans. Do you can all beans the same?

Also, if I wanted to add onions, green pepper and a little olive oil, would that affect the processing time? Thanks for sharing all your great knowledge.

Nancee Quinn, Texas

Yes, you can home can all types of dry beans using the same method, as you outlined. I would not advise soaking peas that long before canning them, though; they'll get mushy. Only soak them for about an hour, then can them up; the canning will finish softening them up. They require a much shorter soaking time than do beans. Some tiny beans, such as tepary beans and lentils, also require a shorter soaking time, due to their size.

Personally, I'd use very little olive oil; when you can, sometimes oil works out under the lid and prevents it from sealing. But that and the onions and peppers and/or spices will not affect the processing time. Enjoy!

Canning dry lentils

Do you have a recipe for canning dry lentils? I have about 20 pounds that I bought for 25 cents a pound.

Joyce Pierce, Alabama

Lentils can be canned up using any recipe for canning dry beans. They are small and cook up quite quickly, so overnight pre-soaking is not necessary.

Put lentils into a large pot and cover with at least two inches of hot water. Bring to a boil. Simmer about 10 minutes, then pack lentils into pint canning jars, leaving two inches of headspace. Fill the jars with the boiling cooking water, leaving 1 inch of headspace. Add 1 tsp. salt, if desired. Process pints for 75 minutes at 10 pounds pressure. If you live at an altitude above 1,000 feet, consult your canning book for directions on increasing your pressure to suit your altitude, if necessary.

Syrup, coffee, and dry mixes

Canning maple syrup

Fall has finally arrived and I have been wondering about canning maple syrup. I have seen many recipes to make it, but have not seen any canning recipes. Is maple syrup something that can be canned?

Leigh Ann Mitchell, Texas

Yes, you can home can maple syrup. After boiling down maple syrup and filtering it, heat it to 190°F in a double boiler (or one large kettle inside another, with the larger one containing water to prevent scorching). Then pour off into hot, sterilized canning jars and process in a boiling water bath canner for 10 minutes.

Ask Jackie

Canning coffee beans

I have an opportunity to buy some great coffee in roasted whole bean form at a great price. It is at such a good price because it is right at the expiration date. I bought one and it tastes great still. What do you think? I was thinking about stocking up on a bunch of it and trying to can it up in jars to keep it longer since it is in a bag right now. Is this a good idea, and if so should I can it ground up or in beans and how?

Jessica Koerner, Indiana

To tell the truth, I've never canned coffee. But if I were to give it a try, I'd can it in whole beans, using the time and method used for canning nutmeats. All I can say is to give it a try and see how it works. Then you can let everyone know how it went after a year's time. It should work fine.

To can nutmeats, lay them out on a cookie sheet and heat in the oven at its lowest setting, stirring from time to time to prevent scorching. This usually takes about 30 minutes. Pack hot into hot, sterilized jars and place a hot, previously simmered lid on the jar (not a wet lid!) and tighten the ring down firmly tight. Do *not* add liquid! Process in a pressure canner at 5 pounds for 10 minutes.

Canning coffee drinks

My question is about canning coffee drinks. You know the really expensive ones that you pick up while you're out and about in town? I'd like to make some up in pint jars so I could pull one out of the refrigerator to take with me. I

184

like my coffee with cream or milk. That's what leads to the question. Would I can it like I would milk?

Kimberly Marsh

Boy, Kim, you've got me there. Bob and I hate coffee. No, we're not weirdos or purists; we just don't like the stuff. How 'bout it fellow canners? Anyone out there home can coffee drinks? If so, please write so Kimberly can join you in enjoying her favorite beverage.

Canning dry mixes and breads

Is there a foolproof way of canning dry mixes like cookie mixes and other "just add water" mixtures? I have heard that using oxygen absorbers are good enough in regular canning jars, but the cans just don't "snapseal" like when canning. Also, do you have a good recipe for Boston brown bread which can be canned in canning jars, and how long do canned "breads" like banana nut last in food storage?

Jered B.

I do not can my dry mixes. I simply mix up big batches and keep them in airtight gallon jars until I need some. Of course, these could get rancid after very long-term storage, but mine don't last that long. I regularly use these mixes and then replace the mix when it runs out with fresh.

Any recipe for Boston brown bread may be canned; just fill wide-mouth jars ⅔ full of the batter, allowing for rising during baking. The canned breads seem to stay good indefinitely. I recently ate a Korean War tinned K ration of pound cake and it was fine (and I'm still alive!). I do love to experiment!

185

Ask Jackie

Canning lard

Can you can freshly rendered lard? I'm thinking that it can be done just like butter.

It makes the best pie crust and is a great addition to homemade soap.

Kristine Farley, Washington

To can lard, ladle the hot lard into hot, sterilized wide-mouth jars, leaving only ¼ inch of headspace. Immediately wipe the rim and place a hot, previously simmered lid on the jar and screw down the ring firmly tight. You can water bath the jars, but they will seal without it. This lard is good for years without becoming rancid.

Jackie Clay has inspired thousands of readers with her articles in *Backwoods Home Magazine* with her perseverance, homesteading knowledge, and wisdom. When you read this book you step into Jackie Clay's world along with her readers who watch this modern day pioneer carve a home in the wilderness.

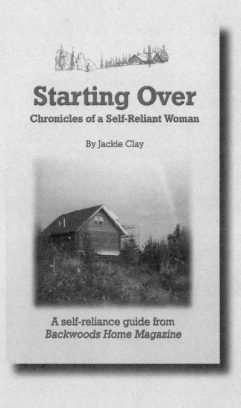

Starting Over
Chronicles of a Self-Reliant Woman

By Jackie Clay

A self-reliance guide from
Backwoods Home Magazine

Ask Jackie

**If you like this book,
you'll also like Jackie's**

Growing and Canning
Your Own Food

**What kinds of food to have in your pantry.
How much to have in your pantry.
Recipes to use your preserved foods.**

Jackie Clay's
Pantry Cookbook

Other titles available from Backwoods Home Publications

The Best of the First Two Years
A Backwoods Home Anthology—The Third Year
A Backwoods Home Anthology—The Fourth Year
A Backwoods Home Anthology—The Fifth Year
A Backwoods Home Anthology—The Sixth Year
A Backwoods Home Anthology—The Seventh Year
A Backwoods Home Anthology—The Eighth Year
A Backwoods Home Anthology—The Ninth Year
A Backwoods Home Anthology—The Tenth Year
A Backwoods Home Anthology—The Eleventh Year
A Backwoods Home Anthology—The Twelfth Year
A Backwoods Home Anthology—The Thirteenth Year
A Backwoods Home Anthology—The Fourteenth Year
A Backwoods Home Anthology—The Fifteenth Year
A Backwoods Home Anthology—The Sixteenth Year
A Backwoods Home Anthology—The Seventeenth Year
A Backwoods Home Anthology—The Eighteenth Year
A Backwoods Home Anthology—The Nineteenth Year
A Backwoods Home Anthology—The Twentieth Year
A Backwoods Home Anthology—The Twenty-first Year
A Backwoods Home Anthology—The Twenty-second Year
A Backwoods Home Anthology—The Twenty-third Year
A Backwoods Home Anthology—The Twenty-fourth Year
A Backwoods Home Anthology—The Twenty-fifth Year
A Backwoods Home Anthology—The Twenty-sixth Year
A Backwoods Home Anthology—The Twenty-seventh Year
A Backwoods Home Anthology—The Twenty-eighth Year
A Backwoods Home Anthology—The Twenty-ninth Year

About the author

Jackie is a lifelong homesteader. From the tender age of three, she dreamed of having her own land, complete with chickens and horses. Learning life skills such as canning, gardening, and carpentry from her mother, father, and grandmother, she slowly became a very experienced homesteader. She has more than 45 years of experience foraging wild foods, growing a garden, raising homestead animals such as goats, cattle, horses, pigs, and, of course, chickens. Jackie cans hundreds of jars of gourmet-quality, homegrown food every single year. The family eats like kings!

She lives on a wilderness 120-acre homestead with her husband, Will (also a lifelong homesteader), and son, David. They raise nearly 90% of their own food and strive for a more self-reliant, off-grid lifestyle.

Jackie has written for many years for *Backwoods Home Magazine*, doing both feature articles on all aspects of low-tech homesteading as well as the informative Ask Jackie column since 1999. She also maintains a popular "Ask Jackie" blog at the magazine's website, www.backwoodshome.com/blogs/ JackieClay. She has also written several books including *Growing and Canning Your Own Food, Jackie Clay's Pantry Cookbook,* and *Starting Over,* as well as several more on animal care.